WRAP IT UP

To Ilana
Best wishes...
and happy wrapping!

Antonia
'99

WRAP IT UP

ARONA KHAN

WARD LOCK LIMITED · LONDON

For Hélène and Sam Khan, my dear parents, with love.

© Arona Khan 1987
© Photography and line drawings Ward Lock Limited 1987

First published in Great Britain in 1987
by Ward Lock Limited, 8 Clifford Street,
London W1X 1RB, an Egmont Company

Text filmset/set in 12/13 Bauer Bodoni
by Tradespools Ltd, Frome, Somerset

Printed and bound in Italy
by Sagdos

British Library Cataloguing in Publication Data

Khan, Arona
Wrap it up — (Living style series).
1. Gift wrapping
1. Title II. Series
745.54 TT870

ISBN 0-7063-6558-5

CONTENTS

INTRODUCTION

When I was three-and-a-half years old my grandmother came to visit us. Not very exciting? Well it was for her when after a few days her knickers disappeared. Eventually they were discovered, all made into neat little parcels. I had begun gift-wrapping!

Since I was old enough to use a pair of scissors I have enjoyed wrapping real presents (as against procured panties!). Along the way I have also learnt that the effort you put into the presentation of a gift can be as much appreciated by the recipient as the contents. Carefully choosing a gift and then using too much paper and tape to wrap it is like buying a beautiful outfit and wearing it under a tatty old coat.

Gift-wrapping is not difficult. It just needs a little thought, time and practice. This book has been written, not so much as a manual, but more as a guidebook to show you the routes I have found to successful wrapping, so that soon, and with greater confidence, you will try out your own variations on my themes.

Start by looking through the alphabetical list of equipment in 'Down to basics' to decide what you will need for your starter kit. Quite soon you could start to adopt 'squirrel' tendencies, hoarding useful items found about the home. Plastic fruit and vegetable trays from the supermarket, for example, will get a new lease of life. You could also find yourself wandering through specialist paper stores searching for alternative gift-wrapping materials.

If you are particularly interested in making cards and tags, or designing your own paper, you'll soon discover that artists' supply shops offer a marvellous selection of card, paper and colouring pencils; some pencils are even water soluble for extra versatility. You'll also have a huge choice of felt-tip pens. These come in different colours and tip widths, and you should be able to find italic felt-tip pens, metallic markers, metallic outlining pens, and fluorescent poster markers quite easily. With health and safety in mind you'll notice that a lot of these pens are now non-toxic and odourless.

If children are going to be helping you, make sure they use specially-designed paper scissors and non-toxic felt-tip colouring pens with caps that can't be swallowed. Pens with ink made from food colouring are a particularly good idea as any marks can be easily washed out.

You may not want to read this book from cover to cover, preferring, instead, to 'dip into' it from time to time to see how to wrap a particular gift. To begin with however, read 'Wrap it up'. This information forms the foundation of the gift-wrapping knowledge you will build on through subsequent chapters.

Once you find out how easy it is to decorate your gifts by making pleats or bows, 'Dressing up' could become mildly addictive! In 'Tagging along' you will soon see why it's worthwhile keeping all sorts of odds and ends of paper, card and other materials. With very little effort you can turn them into gift tags or cards, greeting cards, and even envelopes. In 'Cover-up' you will see how it takes little more than a sheet of paper to turn even the tattiest empty box into terrific 'wrapping' for a fragile present or a last-minute gift.

Please handle the pages of 'It's a problem' with care as they may wear out with overuse! Here you'll discover how a few simple instructions mean many presents are no longer problem packages.

Cellophane seems to be an ideal way to wrap many of your home-made or home-grown gifts as you'll find out in 'Home is where the art is!'. Finally, there are some original ways to wrap gifts or make tags for those special occasions in 'It's a celebration'.

Please read all instructions carefully at least once before starting to wrap, and then *follow* them! Exact measurements have not been given, as these will differ according to the size of each gift. After all, presents come in all shapes and sizes! Don't panic if the results aren't exactly as you would desire at first – with a little practice you will soon amaze yourself!

Whether you are hoping to prevent your gift-wrapping efforts looking as though they have been put through a spin dryer, or if, more specifically, you want to find out how to wrap a bottle or some other difficult shape such as a ball or a triangular box, this book will help you to achieve stunning results.

1 DOWN TO BASICS

Even if your interest in needlework extends no further than sewing a button on a shirt, you no doubt have a sewing kit at home, and if your DIY skills only go as far as changing a plug, you probably have a tool-kit of sorts in the cupboard. So what about starting a 'bits box' for gift-wrapping? That way you have all the materials to hand when you need them and it saves you having to turn the cat out of its basket while you play hunt the ribbon yet again! An old shoe-box would be ideal; it could, after all, prove a little difficult to rush around the house with a drawer under your arm every time you seek space and sanctuary to avoid prying eyes seeing their presents prematurely!

Once you have organized where you are going to keep the 'bits', give some thought as to what you might put in the box. You won't need to buy everything. Some things you will find about the home and you can build up your supply of other materials gradually. Here is a list to start you off:

Adhesive Check that the adhesive you buy, in stick or liquid form, is suitable for use on card and paper. Use it particularly for fixing decorative extras such as glitter and paper shapes to gifts and tags.

Boxes These will prove a little difficult to keep inside your 'bits box', instead try to keep a selection tucked away on top of a wardrobe or under the bed. Those with separate lids can in no time at all become handsome present carriers (see Cover-up, page 43). Keep a selection as they will come in useful, particularly when wrapping awkward-shaped or fragile gifts. To save space, store boxes inside each other.

Cardboard Cardboard should be kept, be it corrugated or flat (as found in packets of tights and shirts, or at the back of note-pads), as it makes wrapping difficult shapes such as clothes so much easier (see It's a problem, page 56).

Cellophane This is the answer to many of your problems, especially when you are wrapping food, plants or home-grown produce (see Home is where the Art is!, pages 62–67).

Compass Blow the dust off your old pencil case and see how a compass is a lot less cumbersome and more accurate than using a saucer or eggcup to draw a circle or curve. A protractor will also help you to get the shape right.

Double-sided tape You will find this invaluable! It ensures extremely neat wrapping and is also very economical if you buy a large roll. You don't need to use the full width of a strip; it is often easier to cut it into shapes that best suit your needs.

Empty cartons Plastic containers with lids, the kind that originally contained ice-cream or margarine, are very useful for storing odd shapes of ribbon (which will come in useful later when decorating tags) and other bits and pieces. The trays found in biscuit packets or chocolate boxes which are divided into sections are also handy if you want to keep colours or shapes separate.

Flowers Fresh and dried flowers can add a lovely touch to your gift-wrapping (make sure the fresh flowers are put in water once the present has been opened). Keep and later use the floral sprays which sometimes decorate boxes of chocolates.

Glitter and cardboard or paper shapes are just a couple of ways to decorate wrapped presents, gift tags and cards. Remember to place the item on a sheet of paper before using adhesive and glitter on it, so that the excess glitter can be poured back into the container. This will prevent the carpet from starting to glisten! Look out for self-adhesive plastic shapes in the shops.

Hole punch Gift tags take on a more professional look if they have a neat hole punched in a corner through which the ribbon or cord can be tied. Other attempts to make a hole using the tip of a pencil or scissors can result in the tag looking as though the dog has tried to take a bite out of it! Keep the punched out circles of card in your 'bit box' for decorating tags.

Invisible tape or ordinary clear tape are excellent when it is too awkward to use the double-sided variety; for example, on the underside of a bottle. When using invisible tape, remember to rub it into the paper to ensure that it cannot be seen. In case of emergency, invisible or clear tape can be folded back and used in place of double-sided tape.

Junk jewelry A broken pearl necklace or single diamanté ear-ring need not end up being discarded. Instead it can make the wrapping of an anniversary present, for example, look stunning, and it also shows that you put a lot of thought into the decoration as well as the gift.

Knife Cutting out cardboard shapes is easier and very accurate results are achieved if a safety knife or scalpel is used. But remember to place a board or some other protection beneath the card to prevent your work from being forever etched on the dining-room table! Keep your knife well out of the reach of children and choose one with a retractable blade or protective cap.

Labels Even sticky labels have a part to play in gift-wrapping (see Home is where the art is!, pages 62–67)

Lace Thirteen can be lucky for some, especially if you wrap their anniversary present in lace (see It's a celebration, page 71).

Metal ruler If you often use a scalpel or safety knife to cut out cardboard shapes against the straight edge of a ruler, one made of plastic or wood would soon look as though it was growing teeth as more and more dents appeared in the sides. A ruler made of plastic or wood, however, comes in very handy whether you are measuring card to make a gift tag or are working out the dimensions of a Cover-up box.

Off-cuts Save pieces of ribbon, card, cellophane, wrapping or tissue-paper . . . in fact, everything! No matter how small they are, they can be used to make original decoration on gift tags, etc.

Pens A selection of felt-tip pens are always useful, either when designing your own wrapping paper or for decorating tags and cards. Gold, silver and other metallic-coloured pens may cost a little more, but the results can be spectacular.

Polystyrene chips Fragile objects packed in boxes can be protected by polystyrene chips, or use some bubble wrap.

Ribbon offers endless ways of decorating your gift-wrapping (see Dressing up, pages 28–34). To begin with, select just a few colours and then gradually add others to your collection. If possible try to buy large rolls of synthetic ribbon as it is much more economical. Sometimes it's luxurious to use real ribbon, so watch out for cheap remnants of velvet or satin.

Scissors A sharp pair of scissors will ensure the edges of your wrapping paper don't look as though they have been cut with a blunt bread knife! Please be very careful to keep scissors out of the way of children who, if they are helping you, should use a pair of specially-designed children's paper scissors.

A pair of pinking shears can be used to give a zigzag pattern to your bows, or for trimming the paper around the top of a bottle or at the ends of a cracker, or to turn old greeting cards into natty new gift tags (see Tagging along, pages 35–42).

Stapler When making bows and other decorations a small stapler is easier and less fiddly to use than sticking lots of bits of ribbon together.

Tissue-paper This has many uses, for example facilitating the wrapping of awkward-shaped gifts (see It's a problem, pages 48–61).

Vegetable or fruit trays from the supermarket or greengrocer can become very smart and inexpensive 'baskets' (see Home is where the art is!, page 62).

Wrapping paper To avoid pre-party panics keep a selection of papers which will cover most occasions. Don't forget that some designs will be suitable for a multitude of events (e.g. a heart pattern could be used for engagements, weddings, anniversaries and, of course, St Valentine's Day). Wrapping paper can be expensive so look out for sale bargains. Left over pieces of paper, no matter how tiny, are worth saving for decorating. The smaller pieces can also be used to wrap little gifts or to make co-ordinating tag envelopes (see Tagging along, page 35). You will find out more about the types of paper available in Wrap it up (see page 12) and also how to decide which paper is best to use for various shaped gifts and for different occasions. When buying sheets of wrapping paper always ask for it to be rolled rather than folded. It can, however, work out more economical to buy rolls of wrapping paper, and the cardboard roll protects the paper from getting crushed.

Yarn If you knit a gift and have some wool left over, use it to decorate the wrapping instead of ribbon.

2 WRAP IT UP

Neither your knees, the edge of the bed, the carpet nor the front seat of the car are where you should wrap a present. You must use a clean, dry, flat surface, like a table or a work-top in the kitchen, with a reasonable amount of clear space so that you can work comfortably. Trying to wrap a package through a mountain of ironing or a pile of dirty plates does nothing for your creativity!

CHOOSING WRAPPING PAPER

There is such a wide variety of paper available that you are spoilt for choice. However, when making your selection bear in mind both the shape and size of the gift. A large pattern on a small box is wasted because you can't see most of it. Equally, a tiny pattern is lost on a gigantic box. A gift wrapped with plain paper is more likely to need some kind of decoration, whereas a patterned paper may look interesting enough on its own.

Lightweight paper

Non-geometric patterned paper (a floral design for example) makes wrapping difficult shapes much easier as it is more flexible than, say, thick glossy paper. A thick glossy paper would become a sea of 'veins' where the gloss cracks at the folds but with a patterned lightweight paper the creases won't show up. If the paper is very thin, check that the pattern on the box won't show through. To counteract such a problem, wrap the gift in tissue-paper before covering with wrapping paper.

Heavyweight paper

This is best used when wrapping something that has sharp edges such as a box. If you use it on a gift with curves, the gloss cracks on the surface resulting in a series of random lines or 'veins'. Glossy patterned paper is ideal for a Cover-up box because the gloss not only gives it a rich look, but also protects the cover from getting easily marked.

TYPES OF WRAPPING PAPER

Wrapping paper is widely available at gift and stationery shops and department stores. It is also worth looking around them or art supply shops for other wrapping materials. Below are some to look out for.

Tissue-paper comes in a variety of colours. It is widely available in shops, but you can also save sheets from purchases made at clothes shops, off licences, etc., and iron them out if you don't like the crumpled look but only use a very cool iron setting. You can use tissue-paper to cover a gift before you gift-wrap it – either because the pattern on the gift will show through the wrapping paper otherwise or because it will look even nicer with a double wrap, for example if you are wrapping lingerie. Or wrap a present in a few sheets of different coloured tissue-paper to give a rainbow effect.

Tissue-paper also makes good 'packing' material for fragile or odd-shaped gifts in a box. If you have access to a paper shredder you can make inexpensive but pretty packing by using either single or multi-coloured tissue-paper.

Crêpe paper is inexpensive to buy and comes in a wide range of colours. Because of its flexibility, it is without doubt the answer to your problems if you are wrapping a ball shape or a curved bottle, or if you are making a cracker. It is best to secure crêpe paper by tying it, as it does not stick to adhesive tape easily. Crêpe paper is not a good choice if you are likely to get it wet (in the rain?) as it marks easily.

Foil or metallic paper Very lightweight sheets of *paperbacked foil* can be used as box lining while a heavier weight foil paper is more suitable to wrap with, as it creases well when pleated. *Metallic PVC* in sheet form is now becoming widely available. This is a plasticized silver foil, sometimes with a patterned overlay. It is very slippery and is best used to cover a box that you will be decorating with ribbon as it is difficult to fold or pleat. But be warned – it is a bit like wrapping with a wet fish! *Rainbow (prismatic) acetate* is also very slippery but has an interesting 3D quality as the pattern on the sheet catches the light. You can buy sticky-backed, prismatic-patterned, *diffraction foil* by the metre, and even small pieces can be kept to create a dazzling decoration. *Crinkle foil*, like crêpe paper, makes wrapping curved shapes simple. Just half a metre of ribbed *ribbon foil* will enable you to make some eye-catching bows. Keep off-cuts of all these materials to decorate gift tags.

Marbled paper is normally medium to heavyweight and is easy to wrap with as it creases well. It is best used for sharp outlines, like boxes, as it is not very flexible.

Flock paper has a felt-like quality and can be bought by the metre in a variety of colours. You can make attractive and long-lasting Cover-up boxes, especially for children, with this paper.

Satinwrap is actually large sheets of synthetic ribbon which come in a wide range of colours, either plain or with a gold or silver patterned overlay. Although the cost is the same as an average sheet of wrapping paper, satinwrap can be a lot more versatile either for gift-wrapping or decoration. You can be really creative and mix colours of the ribbon and wrapping.

Satinwrap is easiest to use on cylindrical bottles or box shapes, so long as you don't want to fold or pleat it much. It requires just a little practice and a lot of adhesive to fix in place. You can tear strips off the sheets though they will not always be of equal width from top to bottom, so it is best to use scissors if you want accuracy. Try using pinking shears for some interesting effects.

Cellophane is now available in various thicknesses, colours and designs. Transparent lightweight cellophane is great for wrapping plants or flowers (see It's a problem, page 58) and this or iridescent cellophane – iris film – is perfect for covering difficult-shaped gifts (see It's a problem, pages 48–61). Cellophane can also be used to cover home-made goodies such as *petit fours* (see Home is where the art is!, page 62), or for presentations when you want the recipient and the other guests to see what the gift is without having to open it (see It's a celebration, page 72). Patterned cellophane (or acetate, which is thicker and less flexible), with a snow or heart design for example, can be used as an overlay on wrapping paper.

Card has many uses, whether you are making gift tags or trying to wrap clothing so it doesn't look like it's been sat on, or to disguise an obvious shape, or to make crackers or tree triangles for Christmas, so keep a variety of colours and thicknesses.

You can also find some gift-wrapping materials around the home such as those listed below. Designing your own paper can be great fun too.

Scented drawer lining paper If you happen to have spare sheets of this paper, use it to wrap lingerie or other clothing which will absorb the fragrance. Check first that the recipient doesn't have sensitive skin. Don't wrap food in this paper.

Lightweight wallpaper can make very effective gift-wrapping. Again, because of the thickness of the paper and to avoid 'veining', it is best used for gifts with well-defined edges rather than soft parcels.

Graph paper, newspaper and brown-paper can all make a highly original and personalized gift-wrapping (see It's a problem, page 48).

WRAPPING TIPS

Don't forget to think about how you will be delivering presents when you wrap them. Will they get squashed in a carrier bag en route or will they be buried under the winter woollies you've packed? It may be a good idea to wrap these presents but to keep the decoration separate and fix it on the gift when you unpack; or support the bow with some tissue-paper or a ring of cardboard to prevent it from getting crushed. Alternatively, if you decorate your wrapping with pleats, particularly fan-shaped pleats, it is often attractive enough not to need a bow at all.

If you have a multitude of presents to wrap, stop after a while and take a break, otherwise your gift-wrapping may begin to look a little tired too.

Before wrapping anything bear in mind the following points.

1 To distinguish between the plain and patterned sides of a sheet of wrapping paper, the 'inside' is the plain side and the 'outside' is the patterned side. In the event of the paper being patterned on both sides, choose which should be the 'outside' before you begin wrapping.

2 Both the sides and ends of the paper are folded over for neatness. The sides are folded over before you begin wrapping and the ends are folded before they are sealed to the package with adhesive tape.

3 To crease a line, run both your first fingers firmly along the sheet of paper from the centre to the outer edges. Don't play pat-a-cake with it!

Having said all that, let's get down to the business of wrapping what is possibly the most frequently given gift . . . the box of chocolates. Just one thing before beginning . . . have you taken off the price tag?!!

THE BOX OF CHOCOLATES

You need: wrapping paper; scissors; double-sided tape.

Place the box on the inside of the paper (fig. 1a) and work out how much you need by lightly wrapping the sheet around the box, allowing extra for a small overlap at each side (fig. 1b). At the ends allow paper no more than the depth of the box (fig. 1c) to ensure neat folds. Cut out the paper. If you are using patterned paper, use the pattern as a guide to help you cut straight lines. For neatness fold over both sides, and line up the edges of the sheet at both ends (presuming they are not crooked) to ensure straight overlaps.

Place the box upside down on the inside of the paper, so that when you have finished wrapping, the sealed side

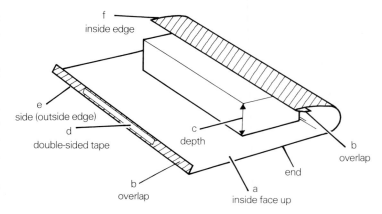

1 Place the box upside down on the paper, which should be inside face up

Birthday surprises come in all shapes and sizes.

will be on the bottom. At this point you might find it helpful to cut some strips of double-sided tape ready for use, but be careful that they don't damage what you stick them to. Fix a length of double-sided tape along one of the folded over sides (fig. 1d). This is now the outside edge (fig. 1e). Remove the backing strip from the double-sided tape. Making sure it is straight, lay the inside edge over the base of the box (fig. 1f). Gently place the taped side on top of it making sure the paper is taut to avoid a baggy wrap.

Keeping the box upside down, turn one end towards you. Fold down the top flap (fig. 2) and crease the sides into triangles. This end now looks like an armchair (or a sofa if it's a wide box!). Firmly fold both sides towards the centre (fig. 3a). Before turning up the base, fold over

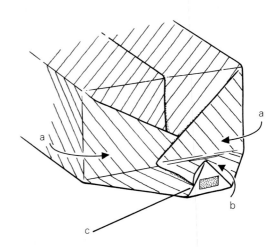

3 Make sure the paper is taut as you seal the base triangle in position

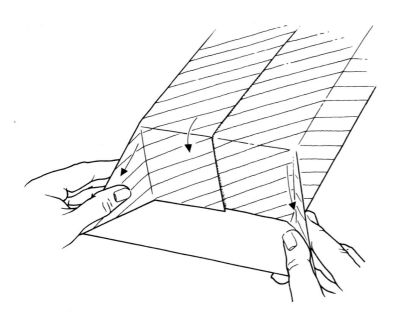

2 Fold down the top flap to make an armchair shape

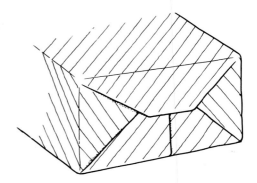

4 The end result

its tip (fig. 3b) to give a neat edge and fix double-sided tape along the inside edge (fig. 3c). Remove the backing strip and, keeping the paper taut, lift and press it against the end of the box.

With the other end facing you, repeat the folding process. Turn the box right side up and hey presto – the perfect package (fig. 4).

3 DRESSING UP

It's time to start thinking about decorating your wrapping. There are a number of ways to make a simple gift look special; for instance, by pleating the paper, or by adding some ribbon or a bow. In this chapter there's an abundance of bows and plenty of pleats, with simple instructions and drawings to guide you. Remember, these are just suggestions. If you devise a method that you find easier, follow it. Just one word of warning – bow-making can become addictive!

PLEATING

The wonderful thing about pleating is that you can't be right or wrong. Once you've learnt the basic methods – just use your instincts as to what you think will look good.

Pleats can go along the length of a parcel or they can go right around it. They can be fan-shaped or inverted. They can be part of the sheet used for wrapping or they can be cleverly fixed on when the wrapping is completed. They can vary in width and they don't even need to be made from a matching paper – the same design paper in another colour can be very striking. Pleats on diagonally-lined paper show up very well. As you can see the possibilities are almost endless.

Before we look at the different ways of pleating paper, there are a few pointers to bear in mind.

1 To begin with, it is very important to practice on some spare paper to see how much paper pleating uses up. You can use any paper – some you don't like, brown paper, or even newspaper if you don't mind ending up with your hands covered in print. The size of the paper is up to you, but don't make it too small or you will not be able to see what you are doing. This exercise will help you in future to estimate more confidently how much extra to allow for pleating when wrapping gifts. This will vary according to the size of each present, what type of pleats you want to make, and what size you make them.

2 To work out how much paper you need to wrap a gift, wrap the paper loosely around the parcel, allowing extra for the pleats at one side (for those running lengthwise) or at one end of the paper (for wraparound). Your estimate for inverted pleating will depend whether you are pleating lengthways or widthways around the gift. Fan pleats are made on a separate sheet of matching or co-ordinating paper.

3 Except for fan-shaped pleats, always remember to align pleats with both edges of the sheet of paper (presuming they are straight!) to ensure that they run parallel, or you will end up with fan pleats whether you want them or not!

4 When turning a sheet of paper over in these instructions, always turn it sideways as if you were turning the pages in a book. Otherwise you could end up with your pleats and folds facing the wrong way.

5 If you want the pleats in the middle of the sheet, start folding the paper about one third of the way in.

Lengthwise pleats: practice

These pleats run along the length of a gift.

You need: paper; scissors; adhesive tape.

Cut out a piece of paper and place it inside facing up, with one side in front of you. Fold one edge of the paper over (as wide as you want the first pleat to be (fig. 5). Fold it over again and run your fingers along the line to crease it (fig. 6). Turn the paper outside facing up and make a fold half the width of the pleat away from you (fig. 7).

Turn the paper inside facing up and fold it away from you as wide as you want the second pleat to be. Crease the line. Turn the paper outside facing up and make a half fold away from you.

Repeat until you have the number of pleats you want.

With the paper inside facing up, fix a couple of strips of invisible tape across the pleats horizontally to seal them in place.

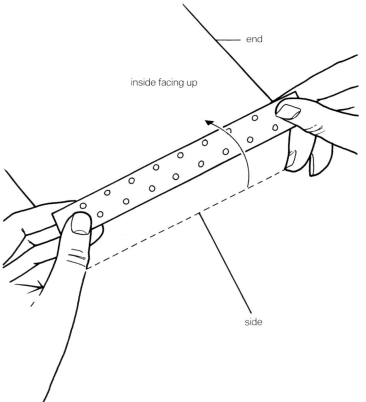

5 Practising lengthwise pleating: with the paper inside facing up, fold it away from you

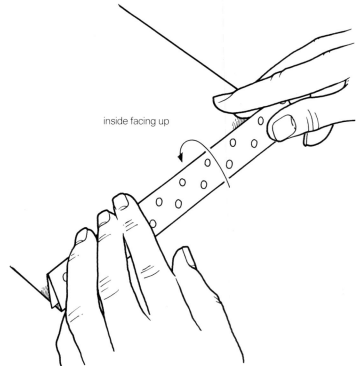

6 Fold the paper over again, as wide as you want the first pleat to be

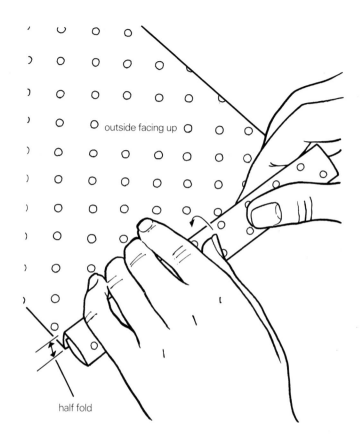

half fold

outside facing up

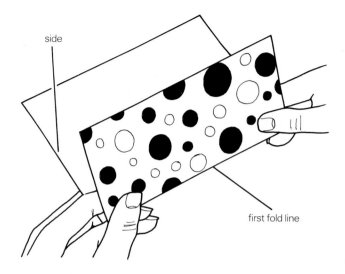

side

first fold line

8 Practising wraparound pleating: with the paper inside facing up, fold the paper away from you to get your first fold line

7 With the paper outside facing up, make a half fold away from you to complete the first pleat

Wraparound pleats: practice

These pleats run horizontally around a gift so you need to work in from one *end* as against a side of the paper, to get the pleats in the right place. Remember, when turning the paper over, alway turn it sideways.

You need: paper; scissors; adhesive tape.

Cut out a piece of paper (remember not to make it too small) and place it inside facing up on a flat surface. With one end in front of you, choose how far down the

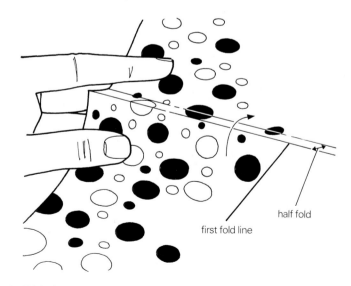

half fold

first fold line

9 With the paper outside facing up, lift the first fold line and make a half fold away from you

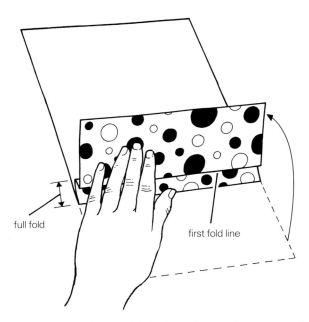

10 Fold the paper (now inside facing up) away from you on the far side of the first fold line

full fold

first fold line

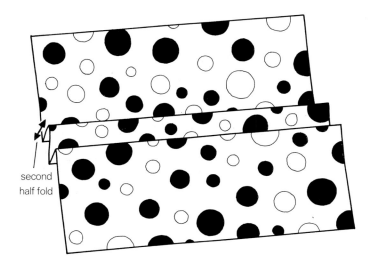

second half fold

11 Making the second half fold

sheet you want the pleating to start. At this point, fold the paper away from you and crease the line (fig. 8). Unfold the paper and lay it outside facing up. Lift the folded line and, working away from you, make a small fold half the size you want each of the pleats to be (fig. 9). Crease the line. Turn the paper inside facing up. Fold the paper away from you on the far side of the fold the width of one pleat (fig. 10). Crease the line. Unfold and lay the paper flat with the outside facing up. Make another half fold (fig. 11). Crease the line. Continue until you have the number of pleats you want. Place the paper inside facing up and seal the pleats in place with invisible tape.

Inverted lengthwise pleats: practice
With inverted pleating, two sets of pleats face each other with a valley running between them. However, the

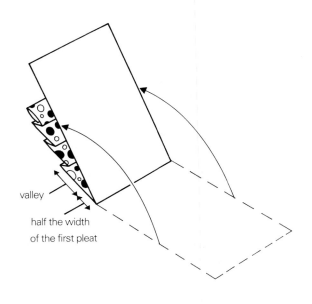

valley

half the width of the first pleat

12 Practising inverted pleating: making the valley

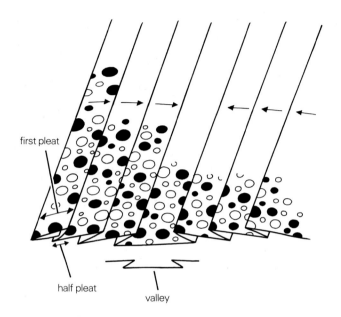

13 *Inverted pleating: the pleats face east and west with the valley inbetween*

number of pleats on either side of the valley do not have to be equal, and an imbalance in the pleats can be made into an attractive feature of the wrapping.

You need: paper; scissors; adhesive tape.

Cut out a length of paper. Make, say, three lengthwise pleats (page 18). With the outside facing up, turn the paper around so that the pleats are now facing you.

With the paper still outside facing up, fold it away from you as wide as you want the valley to be plus half the width of the first pleat (fig. 12). Make a half fold back towards you.

Fold the paper the width of one full fold away from you and a half fold back. Now you have a second pleat (fig. 13). Repeat for the third pleat.

Seal the pleats in place using invisible tape on the inside.

Inverted wraparound pleats: practice
Follow the directions for wraparound pleats (page 19) to your half-way point, then follow the directions as above, from the second paragraph.

Fan pleats: practice
This pleating can be positioned wherever you like on a gift.

You need: paper; scissors; adhesive tape.

Cut out a length of paper and with the inside facing up, make a narrow triangular fold over (fig. 14a) for a neat edge, using one corner as the base point (fig. 14b). Then fold it over again in a large triangular shape (fig. 14c). Turn the paper outside facing up and make a half fold away from you (fig. 14d).

Turn the paper inside facing up and make another

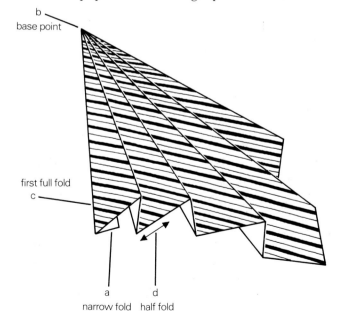

14 *Practising fan pleating: make sure each triangular pleat comes to a sharp point at the base point*

21

Pleats left to right: wraparound (with ribbon), lengthwise, fan, inverted lengthwise (with bow), wraparound (plus card).

triangular fold. Then, outside facing up make another half fold.

Repeat until you have as many pleats as you want in your fan. Fold over the outside edge for neatness and with the paper inside facing up, seal the pleats in place with adhesive tape.

LENGTHWISE PLEATS
(Practice first, page 18)

You will be amazed, delighted even, to see the difference a couple of pleats can make to a wrapped gift.

You need: paper; scissors; invisible or clear tape; double-sided tape.

Measure how much paper you need to wrap the parcel, remembering to allow extra at one side for the pleats. Cut out the paper and place it, inside face up, onto a flat surface. Fold over the edge along one side. This is now the inside edge (fig. 15a). Turn the opposite edge nearest to you.

Depending how wide you want the first pleat to be, fold over the paper twice and run your finger along the crease (fig. 15b). Turn the paper over with the outside face up and make a fold away from you approximately half the width of the pleat (fig. 15c). Crease. Turn the paper inside face up again and make another fold away from you as wide as you want the second pleat to be. Crease the line and turn the paper over, outside face up, and make another half fold away from you. Crease. Repeat until you have the desired number of pleats. Turn the paper inside facing up and hold the pleats in place with strips of invisible or clear tape (fig. 15d).

Place the box on the paper, still inside facing up, and fix a length of double-sided tape along the pleated or outside edge (fig. 15e). Line up the inside edge of the paper with the box. Where exactly you place it will depend on where you want the pleats, so check now that

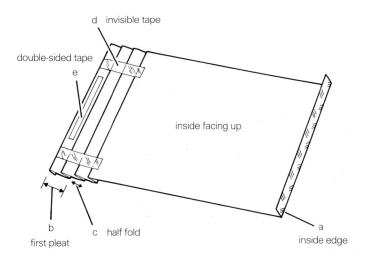

15 *Seal the pleats in position on the inside of the paper using invisible or clear tape*

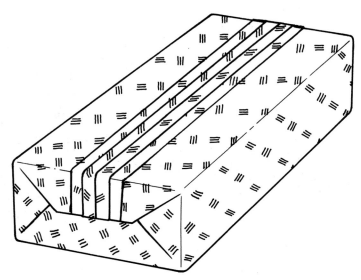

16 *Lengthwise pleats*

when you overlap the pleated side, they will be in the correct position. If you find the pleats are too far over, don't panic. Gently roll the paper round the box until they are in the right position. Remove the backing strip from the tape. Making sure the paper is taut, gently seal the taped edge in place.

Turn the package upside down with one end facing you. Fold down the top flap. This end now looks like an armchair. Firmly fold both sides towards the centre. Before turning up the base, fold over its tip to get a neat edge and fix double-sided tape along the inside edge. Remove the backing from the tape, lift the paper and press it against the end of the box, again keeping the paper taut.

Repeat this process at the other end. Turn the box right side up to discover a perfectly wrapped box with pleats (fig. 16).

WRAPAROUND PLEATS
(Practice first, page 19).

Remember, instead of running along the length of the box, wraparound pleats run around it. Lengthwise pleats are tucked into the 'armchair' folds at each end of the box, but wraparound pleats have to be sealed firmly in place at the edges of the sheet of paper. This type of pleating shows up very well on rectangular boxes. However, it is best to avoid using very thick or glossy paper so that the pleats can be wrapped around the box easily.

You need: paper; scissors; invisible or clear tape; double-sided tape.

Having worked out how much paper you will need (remembering to allow extra at one end for the pleats rather than at the side), cut it out. Place the paper inside face up onto the work surface.

Choose how far down the box you want the pleating to start – always work away from you. For pleats in the middle of the gift, start folding the paper approximately a third of the way from the end of the sheet. Fold the paper over at this point. Crease the line. Unfold the paper and lay it outside face up. Make a half fold away from you. Crease the paper. Turn the paper inside face up again and fold it away from you as wide as you want the first pleat to be on the far side of the creased line. Unfold and lay the paper flat outside face up and make another half fold away from you. Continue until you have the number of pleats you want. Turn the paper inside face up and using invisible or clear tape, seal the pleats in place, especially along the edges (fig. 17a). Fold over the outside edge.

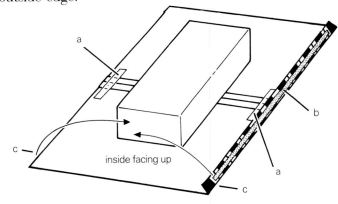

inside facing up

17 Ensure you securely seal the pleats at each edge before wrapping the paper around the gift

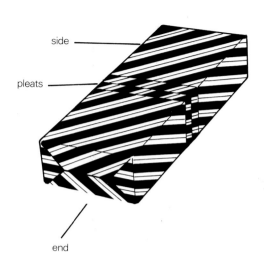

side

pleats

end

18 *Wraparound pleats*

Keeping the paper inside face up, place the gift upside down in position (this way the sealed edge will be on the underside of the gift). Check that the pleats are positioned where you want them in relation to the present. Fix a strip of double-sided tape along one side of the paper (fig. 17b). Remove the backing strip. Making sure the pleats line up, overlap the two sides of the paper (fig. 17c) and press down.

Keeping the box upside down, turn one end of the wrap towards you. Fold down the top flap. This end now looks like an armchair. Firmly fold both sides towards the centre. Before turning up the base, fold over its tip to get a neat edge and fix tape along the inside edge. Remove the backing strip and lift the paper and press it against the end of the box. Keep the paper taut to avoid a baggy wrap.

Repeat this process with the other end. Turn the box right side up to admire another masterpiece (fig. 18).

INVERTED PLEATS
(Practice first, page 20)

Depending whether you want lengthwise or wraparound pleats, follow the appropriate instructions until you reach the halfway point – making the valley. These pleats show up well on a box with a wide surface area (e.g. a square box), but do not use paper that is very heavily patterned or the pleating detail will be lost.

You need: paper; scissors; invisible or clear tape; double-sided tape.

For lengthwise inverted pleats, make the first set of pleats on one side. With the paper outside facing up, turn the sheet around so that the pleats are facing you.

To make the valley fold the paper over away from you. This fold needs to be as wide as you want the valley to be, plus half the width of the first pleat. If you plan to run a strip of ribbon along the valley, it needs to be

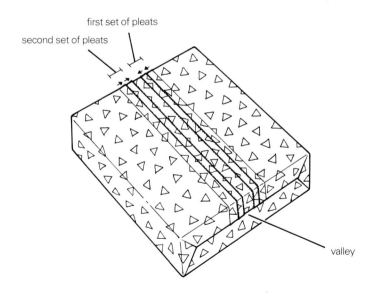

first set of pleats

second set of pleats

valley

19 *Lengthwise inverted pleats*

sufficiently wide for the ribbon to fit. Make a half fold back towards you.

Fold the paper the width of one full fold away from you and a half fold back. Now you have a second pleat. Continue until you have made an equal number of pleats to those on the other side of the valley. Turn the paper inside face up and seal the pleats in place using invisible or clear tape.

Keeping the paper inside face up, place the box on to it and fix a length of double-sided tape along the pleated edge. Remove the backing strip. Line up the opposite side of the paper with the box so that when you seal the pleated side on top of it, the pleats will be in the right place. Seal the taped side down while keeping the paper taut to avoid a baggy wrap.

Turn the package upside down with one end facing you. Fold down the top flap. Firmly fold both sides towards the centre. Before turning up the base, fold over its tip to get a neat edge and fix double-sided tape along the inside edge. Remove the backing strip, lift the paper and press it against the end of the box. Again remember to keep the paper taut.

Repeat this process with the other end. Turn the box right side up to admire your latest success story!

FAN PLEATS

(Practice first, page 21)

Here is a great way to use up leftover paper to decorate a wrapped gift, using a co-ordinating or matching colour or pattern. Fan pleating is the ideal decoration if you are posting the gift or packing it in a suitcase because it lies flat against the package, it cannot get squashed out of shape, unlike a full bow!

When you have completed a basic wrap, the fan pleat can be made separately and then fixed to the wrapping. If the sealed side of the gift is on top, the fan can be tucked under the outside edge or it can cover the seal.

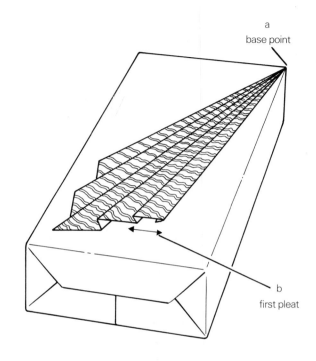

a
base point

b
first pleat

20 *Having completed a basic wrap, seal the pleated paper to the gift in whichever position you prefer. Use double-sided tape.*

Alternatively, have the sealed edge underneath the gift and fix the fan on top at an angle.

A handy rule of thumb regarding the quantity of paper you will need to make a fan pleat is to allow for paper equalling the width and length of the top of the box. A variety of fan shapes can be achieved depending on the size and shape of the paper you use, so do experiment.

You need: paper; scissors; invisible or clear tape; double-sided tape.

With the inside of the paper face up, make a narrow fold so that you have a triangular shape coming to a

Bows left to right: (back) butterfly, full bow, demi-daisy; (centre) curl cluster, twist, snip; (front) roller coaster, paper, crossbow.

point at one corner (fig. 20a). Then fold the paper over again as wide as you want the first pleat to be. Turn the paper outside face up and make a half fold forwards. This is your first pleat (fig. 20b). Continue until you have a series of pleats lying in a fan shape.

Turn the paper inside face up and fix the pleats in place using invisible or clear tape.

The fan pleat can now be sealed to the gift-wrapping using double-sided tape.

Time for another pat on the back!

RIBBONS AND BOWS

Making bows is a bit like knitting – once you know the stitches (or steps in this case) you can do it almost without looking. After a while you will be able to make bows while relaxing, listening to music or watching television. Then when you have a rush of birthdays, there's no panic. The bows are already made. Just wrap the present and seal the bow to it with double-sided tape. But before you get to that stage, remember you can't walk yet, let alone run. So first let's look at the different types of ribbon available.

Velvet or satin fabric ribbon For sheer luxury it is sometimes nice to decorate a gift with real ribbon, and this can be saved and used as a hair decoration once the present has been opened. Or, if you are wrapping a gift in scented paper, decorate it with fabric ribbon which will absorb the fragrance from the paper too. Remember to look out for sale remnants in the stores.

Thin synthetic ribbon is available in a myriad of colours. If possible try to buy large rolls as they are much more economical than small reels. However, those smaller reels are handy if you just need enough of one colour for a particular present. Thin strips of synthetic ribbon make wonderful curl clusters (see page 30).

Wide synthetic ribbon is also on sale in lots of different colours, but it is not normally available in economy sizes. Turn to pages 30–34 to see the beautiful bows it makes.

Satinwrap Sheets of satinwrap can be cut or torn to produce ribbons of any shape or size. Try using pinking shears to cut out lengths of ribbon from the satinwrap. The results can be simply stunning. When you have had a little practice making the bows, experiment by using more than one colour ribbon or by mixing the ribbon widths. For a neat finish, cut out an upside down 'V' shape in the tails of the ribbon lengths.

Lace synthetic ribbon This can be mixed with lengths of coloured ribbon for an eye-catching embellishment.

Patterned synthetic ribbon If you look around the stores you will see a wide selection of ribbons with different designs and messages printed onto them including 'Happy Birthday', 'I Love You', and wedding bells. Also look out for lurex braid.

Sequin scrap or honeycomb trim is not really ribbon at all. It is a shiny, tough, metallic plastic strip from which holes have been punched. It is, in fact, the waste product from making sequins. It can be used to make a brilliant bow (see page 34) and is available from artists' supply shops or shops selling beads or craft materials.

Remember that the design of the paper and shape of the package can affect your choice of decoration. Add the finishing touches to your gift-wrapping either by tying ribbon around it, or by adding a bow, or indeed both. Let's take a look at the possibilities.

CORNERWAYS RIBBON

This works very well on rectangular-shaped gifts. With experience you can use varying widths of ribbon together – e.g. a wide strip in one colour and a narrower strip (cut with pinking shears perhaps) in another colour on top.

You need: ribbon (cut a strip long enough to tie

around the gift twice lengthways – you will have ribbon to spare); scissors; double-sided tape.

Fold the ribbon in half. Place the box upside down on a flat surface. Take the ribbon at its mid point and lay it across one corner of the box. Hold it in place by keeping it between both thumbs and first fingers (fig. 21a). Simultaneously bring each end of the ribbon under the box (fig. 21b), and then up to meet and overlap at the opposite corner (fig. 21c.). Fix double-sided tape to one end of the ribbon and remove the backing strip. While keeping the ribbon taut, place the other end on top of it so that they overlap. Press down firmly. Turn the box right side up.

If you want to add a bow to the ribbon, seal the ribbon on top of the box at one corner. Cover the join by sticking a demi-daisy on top of the seam using double-sided tape.

CRISS-CROSS RIBBON

Ribbon tends to be tied criss-cross around a box with a bow added on top, but how about changing it a little and making the criss-cross off centre without a bow? Again, this works very well on a rectangular box.

You need: Four lengths of ribbon (they can be of different colours and widths; two should be long enough to go around the box widthways and two lengthways, all with an overlap); scissors; double-sided tape.

With the box facing up, take one strip of ribbon and fold it around the box lengthways. Overlap the ends on the underside of the box and seal in place using double-sided tape (fig. 22a). Now tie a length of ribbon widthways around the box (fig. 22b). (Try not crossing the ribbons at the centre point of the box.) Seal it underneath as before.

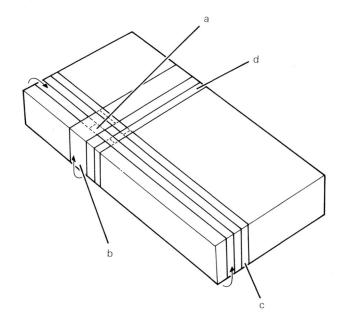

21 *The cornerways ribbon works very well on rectangular-shaped gifts*

22 *Criss-cross ribbons can be in varying widths and colours*

29

Fold the other two ribbons around the box in the same way, one lengthways (fig. 22c) and one widthways (fig. 22d). The final ribbon, however, must be woven under the second lengthways ribbon to keep the criss-cross pattern.

You can also make a more elaborate pattern by adding further strips of ribbon in a continuing criss-cross pattern.

THE STANDARD BOW

You need: a length of ribbon (long enough to tie around the box lengthways and then widthways with some to spare for the bow); scissors.

Place the box upside down on a flat surface. Tie the

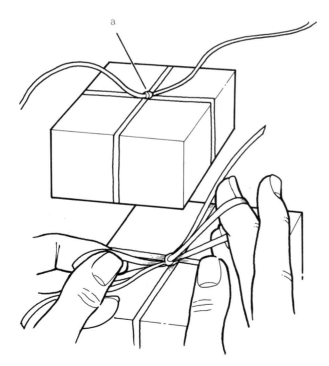

23 *Making a standard bow*

ribbon around the box lengthways and then widthways, and tie the ribbon in a knot at the centre of a criss-cross on the top side of the box (fig. 23a). Make sure when you are tying the knot to hold its centre with your middle finger, releasing your finger at the very last second, to keep the ribbon taut.

Make a bow with the remaining length by taking a loop of ribbon in one hand. Hold it between the tips of your first finger and thumb. With your other hand, take the second strand of ribbon in a circle round the base of the loop, including your thumb, and through the circle to make a second loop. Balance the two loops until they are of equal size. Then hook one loop firmly with your middle finger and pull the other loop, together with the end of the hooked loop, in the opposite direction so that a knot forms in the centre. Hey presto – a bow!

You can trim the ends if they are too long, or you can tie more lengths of ribbon across the centre of the knot to make more bows, perhaps in different colours. This is a handy way to use up odd lengths and colours of ribbon.

CURL CLUSTER

You need: ribbon (at least four lengths, approximately 30 cm (12 in) long, plus one length long enough to tie around the gift criss-cross); scissors.

Tie the long length of ribbon around the gift, lengthways and widthways, and finally knot it on top (fig. 24a). Tie the four strips of ribbon across the knot (fig. 24b) to give you eight half lengths of ribbon. Then, holding a half length of ribbon between your thumb and one of the blades of a pair of scissors (be careful!) (fig. 24c), curl the ribbon by pulling the blade along the ribbon from its base. You now have your first ringlet (fig. 24d).

Repeat for all the half lengths of ribbon. You can divide each strip by tearing still further to make a fluffier bow and curl each of them separately.

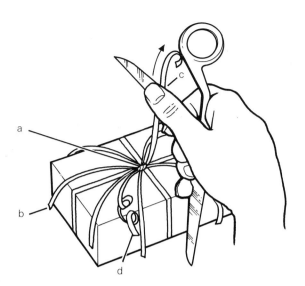

24 *Making a curl cluster*

You will find that some ribbon curls better than others, but be careful to go with the natural flow of the ribbon or you will straighten instead of curl it.

FLAT BUTTERFLY

You need: ribbon (strips approximately 8 cm (3 in) long); scissors; stapler; double-sided tape.

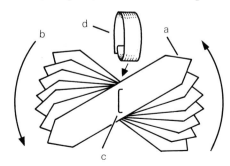

25 *Making a flat butterfly: a useful way of using up odd lengths of ribbon!*

Take the strips (as many as you like, but try it with seven) and cut the ends into points (fig. 25a). Line them up together and then spread them gently into a double-ended fan (fig. 25b). Staple the centre (fig. 25c).

Wrap another strip of ribbon around the centre to make the 'knot' (fig. 25d). Seal the knot at the back with a stapler or invisible tape, and stick to the gift-wrapping using double-sided tape.

DEMI-DAISY

You need: ribbon (length and width will vary according to the size of your gift. Try 70 cm × 1.5 cm (27½ in × ⅝ in)); scissors; stapler; double-sided tape.

Take the ribbon and hold it in one hand. Roll the tip over towards you into a full circle or ring (fig. 26a). Hold it between your thumb and first finger. Make a bottom loop (fig. 26b) and then, by bringing the ribbon up

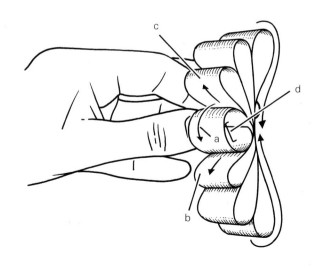

26 *Making a demi-daisy. Make the central ring and loop the ribbon below and above it repeatedly.*

behind the central ring, make a top loop (fig. 26c). Repeat until you have at least two loops at either side of the ring, with each pair increasing in width as you go on. Hold them in place behind the ring and, placing the flat base of the stapler in the ring, staple the back (fig. 26d) thus fixing all the loops in place.

To hide the staple, cover it with double-sided tape, remove the backing and fix a small piece of matching ribbon on top. Stick the bow to your present with double-sided tape.

With a little practice you can make demi-daisies using ribbon in more than one colour or width at a time. A number of variations on the demi-daisy are given below.

The Twist
Make a demi-daisy and hold it in position between the thumb and first finger of one hand prior to stapling it. Gently twist the top half of the loops (the bottom loops will go in the opposite direction). When you have a shape you like, staple the centre of the ring and finish as before.

The Pyramid
Loop the ribbon as for a demi-daisy but this time be extremely careful that they are of equal width and that they lie in a straight line. With the flat base of the stapler in the ring, staple it exactly in the centre of its back, otherwise the pyramid will twist to one side. If your pyramid does twist, this can be overcome by balancing up with another staple if necessary.

Holding your demi-daisy with your first fingers beneath it and your thumbs on top, flatten all the loops starting with the centre and working out. Behold – a pyramid! Finish off and seal to the package as before.

The Crossbow
Make a demi-daisy and then make a second 'daisy' without the central ring. Instead of rolling the tip of the

length of ribbon into a ring, just fold it forwards into the top loop. Then bring the other end of the ribbon back up behind the centre, to make the first bottom loop. Repeat as before. Staple the centre.

Place this 'daisy' crossways under the demi-daisy and, with the flat base of the stapler in the centre of the ring, staple and finish off as before.

FULL BOW
You need: ribbon (try two lengths each approximately 70 × 1.5 cm (27½ × ⅝ in), but this will vary according to the size of your gift); scissors; stapler; double-sided tape.

Roll the tip of one strip of ribbon over towards you into a full circle or ring (fig. 27a). Hold the ring between one

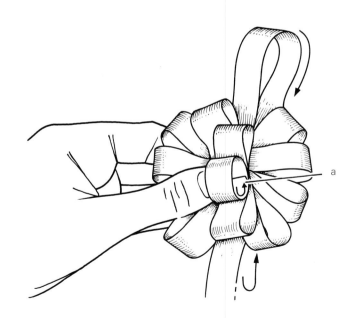

27 A full bow. Build up a series of loops around the central ring, twisting them slightly to form the circular shape.

thumb and first finger. Now build up a series of cross loops at a slight angle to each other. Make them loop backwards and forwards under the ring (as you did for the demi-daisy), but this time twist them slightly until you form a circle of loops. When you have used up the length of ribbon, staple the loops through the back of the central ring. If, however, you find it difficult to hold all the loops in place until the end, staple them in position through the central ring as you complete them, a few at a time.

Hold one end of the second length of ribbon under the centre of the back of the loops and continue making loops as before, stapling in place through the back of the central ring. Cover the staple using double-sided tape and a scrap of the ribbon. Seal to the gift with double-sided tape.

THE SNIP

You need: ribbon (try two lengths each 70 × 1.5 cm (27½ × ⅝ in)); scissors; stapler.

Make a full bow as above. Take a pair of scissors and make angled cuts no more than one third the width of the ribbon on the bend of some of the loops (Fig. 28a). (Take care not to cut right through the loop.) This is a very good way of disguising a failed full bow.

THE ROLLER COASTER

You need: ribbon (try one length of ribbon measuring 70 × 1.5 cm (27½ × ⅝ in)); scissors; stapler; double-sided tape.

Roll the tip of the ribbon forward into a circle. Hold it with your thumb and first finger. Make two more rings around it, each increasing in size. Hold the rings between your two fingers. (Fig. 29a).

Make a small loop on one side of the rings (fig. 29b) and a larger loop on the other side (fig. 29c). Repeat once. Finally, add a small loop on the first side (fig. 29d)

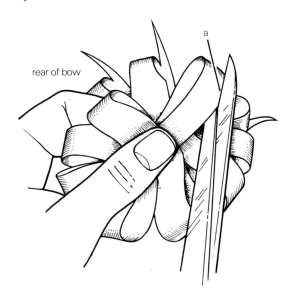

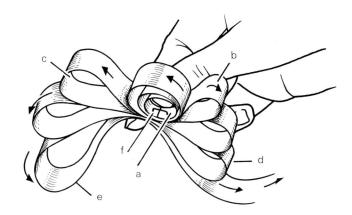

28 Making a snip. A failed full bow can become a successful snip with a few clever cuts from the back to the front of the bow.

29 Making a roller coaster

and a large loop on the other (fig. 29e). Staple the loops in place through the centre of the back of the rings (fig. 29f). Cover the staple using double-sided tape and a scrap of the ribbon as before and seal to the gift with double-sided tape.

SEQUIN SCRAP BOW-TIE

You need: Length of sequin scrap (try 26 × 8.2 cm (10¼ × 3¼ in)); satinwrap (same size as the sequin scrap plus extra for the 'knot' – see below); scissors; clear tape; stapler.

Lie the length of sequin scrap on top of the ribbon (fig. 30a and b). Form them into a circle with the ends overlapping in the middle. Flatten the circle and staple the centre where the ends overlap (fig. 30c). Cut out a bow-tie shape (fig. 30d). Trim the shape if necessary. Cut out a piece of ribbon the width of the centre where the 'knot' should be. Wrap it around the centre and staple at the back (fig. 30e). Cover this in turn with a strip of sequin scrap and seal to the back of the 'knot' using a stapler or clear tape (fig. 30f).

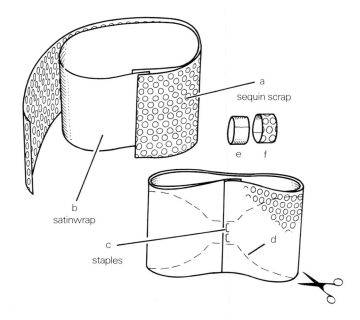

30 *The sequin scrap bow-tie. Placing a layer of satinwrap beneath the sequin scrap not only offers an interesting contrast, but also gives a firm base to staple.*

4   TAGGING ALONG

Single tags, folded tags, gift cards, greeting cards and envelopes are all covered in this chapter. They're inexpensive and fun to make, and are a great way to use up odds and ends of just about everything. All those off-cuts of card, ribbon and paper you've been saving are no longer tagging along. They're about to lead the way to tags and cards galore!

MATERIALS

Card Use all sorts, including old greeting and Christmas cards, calenders, visiting cards, or invitations. It doesn't matter if there is a picture or design you don't like on one side as you can stick plain paper over it. It's important, however, to use the correct adhesive for paper and card and to make sure the edges of the paper are firmly stuck down. Bags of off-cuts are sometimes sold in specialist paper shops so keep a look out.

Ribbon Left-over pieces of satinwrap can be cut into shapes like wedding bells or bow-ties. Strips of ribbon make smart borders on tags too. Lengths of ribbon which are not long enough to make into a bow can be used instead to tie the tag to a gift. Don't forget to experiment using pinking shears for interesting variations.

Wrapping paper What you may previously have thrown out as rubbish can now be used as tag decoration, either to match or co-ordinate with the gift-wrapping.

Pens A message written in ink, or felt-tip pen, or a metallic marker can make a great difference to your tags and cards. Try using dry transfer lettering or stencils to add the finishing touches to an 'execu-tag'. It also avoids confusion, and sometimes embarrassment, if you put initials on the tags if a few people are getting different gifts of a similar shape.

Hole punch Don't keep your hole punch just for making ribbon holes. It can also be used to make interesting patterns. For example, on a folded gift tag or card punch holes in the front and then colour in the circles on the inside of the back of the tag.

Glitter, together with cut-out paper shapes, or self-adhesive plastic shapes like hearts or flowers, are just a few ways to decorate your gift cards and tags. When using glitter, make sure you work on a sheet of newspaper to avoid a mess.

Overlay Fix off-cuts of patterned cellophane or acetate to the front of your cards for a fantastic finishing touch. For example, use snow-patterned acetate for a 'white Christmas'.

MAKING GIFT TAGS AND CARDS

Rather than make tags and cards only when you need them, you may like to spend an evening making a selection, particularly before Christmas or a spate of birthdays or anniversaries. For 'mass production' cover a large sheet of card on one side with thick paper – to cover any picture or writing – and leave it blank to write your message on. Cover the other side of the card with wrapping paper (unless it is coloured card). Cut the sheet into tag shapes and punch a hole in each of them through which you can tie the ribbon. Use a sheet of neutral-coloured card (gold perhaps) to make several ready-made tags for all occasions.

On gift tags and cards, a greeting and your personal message can be written separately. First, write a greeting on the front or back, or inside if it is a folded gift tag or card, e.g. 'Happy Birthday', 'Wish U Better', 'Happy New Year'. See if you can cut out the wording from the wrapping paper. You can also get a striking effect if you write the words in felt-tip pen. Let the ink dry and then dot the letters all over with a metallic marker so they look as though they've got freckles. Then, when you need to send a card or use a tag just write in your personal message.

The Ribbon Tie
This is the easiest way of tying the ribbon through the hole of your tag or gift card.

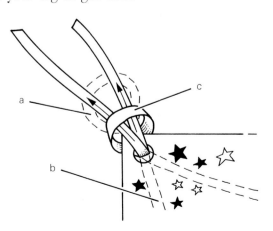

31 The ribbon tie

You need: ribbon (thin strip approximately 30 cm (11¾ in) long); scissors.

Cut a length of ribbon (the size will vary according to your needs). Fold it in half and pull it half-way through the hole in the tag, from the back or plain side through to the front or patterned side, so that the loop (fig. 31a) is on the plain side and the ends (fig. 31b) are on the patterned side. Pull the ends of the ribbon back up through the loop (fig. 31c) and press the knot flat. You can either tie the ribbon around the gift or fix it under a bow or other decoration with invisible tape.

DESIGNING GIFT TAGS AND CARDS

Gift tags and cards can be any shape: square, oval, triangular, round, rectangular, arched, star-shaped, heart-shaped, or for Christmas, stocking or tree-shaped. When deciding what shape to make the tag or gift card, bear in mind the shape of the package. How about a hexagonal tag for a box the same shape? Also consider what the present is for. For example, make a heart-shaped tag for a St Valentine's Day present, but do ensure that you allow enough space both to punch a hole for the ribbon, and write a message; and if you are worried about crooked edges, try cutting the card with pinking shears.

Now let's look at some design ideas for gift tags and cards. Remember, they are just suggestions. Please experiment yourself to see what ideas you can come up with.

Single tags
You need: card; scissors/pinking shears; stick or liquid adhesive; hole punch; ribbon (30 cm (11¾ in) long); decorations.

Example 1 Choose an old greeting card or tag and cut a shape out of the picture on the front. The size of the tag can be varied to suit the size of your gifts; for example, a tiny tag would be unsuitable for a large gift. Try cutting the card out with pinking shears. If there is any handwriting on the back of the card or tag cover it up by sticking a sheet of paper over it, sealing up to the edge with adhesive. Trim the paper to the size of the tag. Punch a ribbon hole in the top left-hand corner, or wherever is most appropriate for the shape of your card. Write your message on the plain side of the card. Tie the ribbon through the hole.

Example 2 Select a sheet of coloured card. Cut out a shape, for example, a star or heart. This can either be done freehand or by tracing the shape onto grease-proof paper. Cut out the grease-proof paper template and place it on the card. Trace around it with a pencil and then cut the shape out. Punch a hole and tie the ribbon through it. Write a message on the back.

Example 3 (Fig. 32). Take a piece of card that is blank on one side. If using card which is dark on both sides, cover one side with white or a pale-coloured paper, so that you can write a message onto it. Then look at the design on the wrapping paper you have used to cover the present and decide which part of it would make the best design on the tag. Try to avoid the 'magician's touch' – cutting characters in half! Cut out the shape and stick it to the card using liquid or stick adhesive. You can also use this method when cutting a shape from an old greeting card or tag. Try outlining the shape on the tag using a coloured pen (fig. 32a). Punch a hole and tie the ribbon through it, and write a message on the back.

Example 4 Use an off-cut of card. It doesn't matter if there is writing on one side. Take a scrap of the paper you used to wrap the gift and completely cover the writing by sticking it to that side of the card. Use pinking shears or scissors to cut out the shape you want. Punch a hole and tie a ribbon through it. Write a message on the back.

Example 5 (Fig. 33) Take a piece of card, plain on both sides. Cut it out to the desired shape and then decorate the 'front', using off-cuts of co-ordinating or matching paper used in the gift-wrapping (fig. 33a).

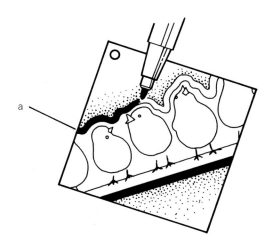

32 Making a single tag using an off-cut from the gift-wrapping paper

33 A single tag – the ideal way to use up odds and ends of ribbon and paper

By using felt-tip pens and odds and ends, card becomes a smart tag and paper a designer wrap.

You can also add other bits of ribbon (fig. 33b), or other decorative pieces. Write the greeting in coloured ink or with a metallic marker (fig. 33c).

Folded gift tags
You need: card; scissors/pinking shears; stick or liquid adhesive; hole punch; ribbon (thin strips 30 cm (11¾ in) long.

Example 1 Take a sheet of card coloured on one side. Fold it in half horizontally or vertically. Cut out whatever shape you like. Write a message on the inside. Punch a hole in the top left-hand corner of the back half of the tag and tie a length of ribbon through it. If you like, you can also decorate the front of the tag.

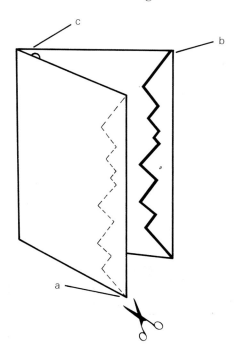

Example 2 (Fig. 34). With card folded in half vertically, cut a pattern on the front of the tag along the right edge (fig. 34a). Outline the shape with a felt-tip pen or metallic marker on the back half of the tag (fig. 34b). Punch a hole in the top left-hand corner of the back half of the tag (fig. 34c) and tie a length of ribbon through it.

Example 3 Choose a piece of card large enough to fold in half, but don't fold it yet. Cover one side in the same paper as you wrapped the gift in. Fold the tag in half with the pattern on the outside front and back. Punch a hole in the top left-hand corner of the back half of the tag and tie a ribbon through it. Write your message inside the tag.

Example 4 (Fig. 35) Fold a piece of card so that the front is shorter than the back. Write a message onto, or decorate, the front portion. Punch a hole in the top left-hand corner of the back half of the tag and tie a ribbon through it.

34 A folded gift tag. Highlight the patterned edge by outlining it on the back half of the tag.

35 Fold the gift tag so that the front is shorter than the back

Example 5 Fold a blank piece of card over and draw or cut out a design – perhaps a cartoon – on the front. Punch a hole in the top left-hand corner of the back half of the tag for the ribbon hole. Write a message inside the tag.

Folded gift cards with envelope
You can make folded gift cards as above, but this time don't punch a hole in the back of the card. Put it in an envelope instead (details for how to make the envelope are given on page 41). Here are some ideas for different designs for a variety of occasions.

Thank you Fold a piece of card in half horizontally or vertically. Write a message or greeting on the front, e.g. 'Thank You!'.

Birthday Fold the card in half vertically. Design the card with a 'bite' out of one corner. Draw a picture of a birthday cake on the front and write a message inside, e.g. 'Happy Birthday'.

Birth congratulations Fold the card in half horizontally. Punch two holes to enable you to tie a bow across the top of the front part of the card (fig. 36a). Write a message beneath the bow, e.g. 'It's a Boy!' (fig. 36).

36 A folded gift card for the birth of a baby. Pull a length of fabric ribbon through the punched holes and tie in a bow at the front.

37 A folded gift card for Christmas. When cutting out the design make sure you leave a small join at the top.

Christmas Fold the card in half horizontally. Cut out a Christmas tree design making sure you leave a small join at the top to hold the card together (fig. 37a). Write a message inside, e.g. 'Seasons Greetings'.

General Fold a piece of card in half either vertically or horizontally. Draw a picture on the front and rule a border around it in coloured ink. Write a message inside.

GREETING CARDS

These are made in the same way as gift cards, except bigger! Here are a few ideas to get you started.

You need: card; scissors/pinking shears; stick or liquid adhesive; decorations.

Christmas Fold a piece of card in half vertically and cut out a design along the outside edge using pinking shears, e.g. a Christmas tree (fig. 38a). Mirror the other

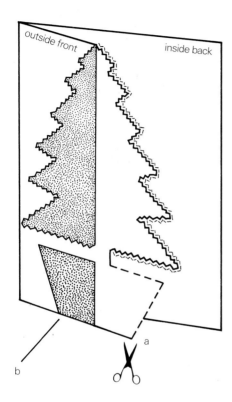

38 A greeting card for Christmas

engagement or wedding you could also add some small hearts and write a message on the bottle label. For the bubbles, decorate the card with glitter.

Bon voyage Fold the card in half horizontally and cut a wavy pattern along the bottom of the front half of the card with the letters BON VOYAGE bobbing on the waves. Decorate the picture with sun and birds.

Easter Fold the card in half vertically. Make an oval shape (for the egg) and draw an Easter bunny inside it. Draw a ribbon around the centre of the egg with a bow tied in front of the bunny's chest. Write 'Happy' and 'Easter' on each half of the ribbon.

AN (EASY!) ENVELOPE

If you can't find an envelope to fit your greeting or gift card exactly, you may want to make one. Co-ordinate your gift-wrapping by making an envelope for your card in the same paper as you used to wrap the gift.

The following measurements are for an envelope to fit a card 9×6 cm ($3\frac{1}{2} \times 2\frac{3}{8}$ in), but which can be adapted for cards of any size.

14 cm (5½ in) wide =	2×6 cm ($2\frac{3}{8}$ in)	front and back of the envelope
	1 cm (⅜ in)	overlap at the side
	1 cm (⅜ in)	extra space
12 cm (4¾ in) long =	1×9 cm ($3\frac{1}{2}$ in)	length of the card
	1 cm (⅜ in)	fold at the top
	1 cm (⅜ in)	seal at the bottom
	1 cm (⅜ in)	extra space

You need: thick paper (or wrapping paper) 14×12 cm ($5\frac{1}{2} \times 4\frac{3}{4}$ in); scissors; pencil; ruler; double-sided tape; stick or liquid adhesive.

half of the design with satinwrap (fig. 38b). Write your message inside the card.

Child's birthday Fold the card in half vertically or horizontally and draw or paint a picture on the front, e.g. a clown with a big bow-tie. Attach an 'age' or 'name' badge, in this example through the 'knot' of the bow-tie.

Congratulations Fold the card in half vertically and draw a bottle of champagne on the front with bubbles and the letters CONGRATULATIONS bursting out from it. If it is to celebrate an occasion like an

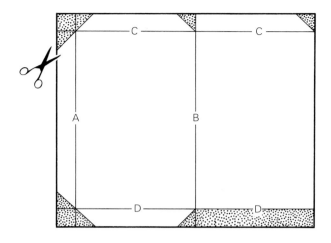

39 *Marking out the measurements onto the paper*

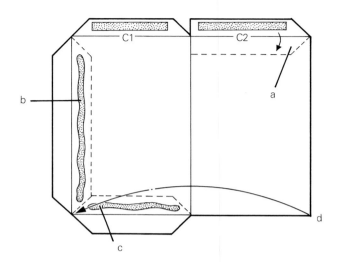

40 *Making an easy envelope*

Lay the paper or card inside face up. Measure 1 cm (⅜ in) in from the left edge and rule a line in pencil lengthways (fig. 39, line A). Then rule another line lengthways 6.5 cm (2⅝ in) in from line A (line B). Along the top of the paper, measure 1 cm (⅜ in) in and rule a border (line C). Repeat along the bottom (line D). Fold over lines A, C, D and B (in that order). Crease and then unfold completely.

Cut off the excess paper (shaded areas of fig. 39).

Fix a strip of double-sided tape to C1 and C2 (fig. 40). Remove the backing strip from C2 and fold the flap over (fig. 40a). Fold over A and D and then run adhesive along both edges of the paper (figs. 40b and c). Press the two halves together (fig. 40d).

Slot your card inside. Remove the backing strip from the double-sided tape on flap C1 and seal the envelope.

5 COVER-UP

In this chapter you will see how easy it is to turn an empty box into the most spectacular problem-solving 'wrap'.

Don't panic because you were meant to be at a party half an hour ago and you haven't even wrapped the present. Cover-up to the rescue. Don't despair if the fabulous present you bought a friend is a dreadfully difficult shape to wrap. Cover-up to the rescue. And just because you'll have to wrap all your presents on Christmas Eve, there is no cause for concern. Cover-up to the rescue once again! What is so good about a Cover-up? They are very cheap and simple to make. They look incredible, and they don't take up much space as they can be stored inside each other. You can make a few at one time and keep them as a standby for the sort of emergencies suggested above. A heart pattern will cover lots of occasions including engagements, weddings and anniversaries. Cover-up boxes for children can be extra fun to make as you can design pictures and patterns on the lid of the box.

Making a Cover-up is as easy as wrapping a present in a box except rather than wrapping up the box as a whole, you cover, separately, both the lid and the base. Don't worry if the box looks a bit tatty or if there is a pattern on it you don't like – heavyweight wrapping paper will literally cover it up! Glossy paper is a good choice here as it will protect the box from getting easily marked. If choosing a thick paper, a flock paper for example, use a box with a loose-fitting lid.

'Wrapping' a gift in this way is ideal if it has to be sent through the post as the box protects the contents. Try not to choose a box that is very heavy as you'll pay for it in extra postage! Keep the packing light by using shredded tissue or polystyrene chips. Then all you need to do is wrap the box in brown paper for mailing.

A RIBBON BAND

One way to keep a Cover-up closed is to slide a decorated ribbon band around it.

You need: ribbon (long enough to go round the box widthways once, plus extra to make a decoration on top); scissors; stapler; double-sided tape.

Wrap the ribbon around the box once. Keeping it as tight as possible, raise the ribbon slightly to place the stapler base beneath it. Staple the band and slide it off the box. Make a demi-daisy (page 31) using the extra ribbon left over. This time start with the wide bottom loops, and finish with the central top loop, through the back of which you can then staple the decoration to the band. You can, of course, make any other bow you prefer. Cover the staple with double-sided tape and place a small piece of the ribbon on top.

CHOOSING A BOX

Small boxes Clever packaging can make inexpensive jewelry look more like the real thing! First take it out of the plastic box or off the card backing it came with. Having covered the lid and base separately, cut wadding (available from the fabric departments in stores) to fit into the base of the box. Place the gift on top. If it is a chain and pendant, first put the chain in the box, then the wadding on top, and, finally, arrange part of the chain with the pendant on top of the wadding. Close the box and add a ribbon band.

Soap boxes These tend to retain the fragrance of the original contents, and are perfect for wrapping clothing, particularly small items such as a scarf or underwear. First wrap the item in tissue-paper, and then place it in the box. Close the box and seal it with a ribbon band. Don't use this type of box for someone who has sensitive skin, or for wrapping food.

Boxes with transparent lids are ideal for wrapping sweets and chocolates, but check first that the box doesn't have a strong smell, of leather for example. Wrap the base as before. Put a layer of thin foil paper in the base, perhaps edged with pinking shears, and a smaller shape cut from a doily on top of it. Put each chocolate in a paper sweet case and arrange them in the box. Close the lid and add a ribbon band.

Medium-sized boxes Old shoe-boxes make handy Cover-ups for slippers and gifts of a similar size. Cover the lid and base of the box. Line the box with a sheet of tissue-paper. Place the slippers inside and cover with the excess tissue-paper. Close and seal with a ribbon band.

Flat medium/large boxes These make gifts of lingerie seem extra luxurious! Having covered the box top and bottom, line it with tissue-paper lengthways and widthways with extra to spare. Place the gift inside and fold the tissue-paper over it. You can add a scented sachet to keep with the lingerie later. For an exclusive touch seal the tissue-paper with a sticker – the recipient's initial perhaps? Close the lid and add a ribbon band round the box.

Spirit boxes A handy way of wrapping a bottle of alcohol is to use a Cover-up box saved from a similar present you received. If it doesn't have a separate lid, cover the outside of the box plus the inside of the lid. Place the bottle inside and seal the Cover-up either with a sticker across the lid and edge of the box top, or with a ribbon band running lengthways around the box. These Cover-ups can also be used to wrap ornaments, such as candlesticks, that don't come in a box. Wrap the ornament first in tissue-paper or bubble plastic and then place it carefully in the box. If it is not securely in place, pad the box with shredded or scrunched up tissue-paper. Seal the box.

Large boxes They can make wrapping a present that consists of lots of pieces easy. Wrap each item loosely in tissue-paper – perhaps mix the colours. Place the wrapped items in the pre-covered box. Close and seal the box. If you don't want to wrap the items individually, pack the gifts in shredded tissue-paper.

Children's boxes You can have lots of fun with these Cover-ups. Plain flock paper, which has a felt-like quality, is a good choice for covering the box. These Cover-ups can double as a treasure chest once the gift has been removed.

MAKING A COVER-UP BOX

You need: an empty box with a separate lid; paper; pencil; ruler; scissors; stick or liquid adhesive.

To work out how much paper is needed, calculate the width across the lid (fig. 41a) and add the depth of both sides doubled (to include the inside of the two sides) plus approximately 1 cm (⅜ in) at each side for an overlap (fig. 41b). (If the height of the side was 5 cm (2 in) and the overlap was 1 cm (⅜ in) your calculation would be $5 \times 2 + 1 = 11$ cm (4⅜ in).) Then work out the length of the lid (fig. 41c) plus the depth of both the ends doubled with again about 1 cm (⅜ in) on each side for

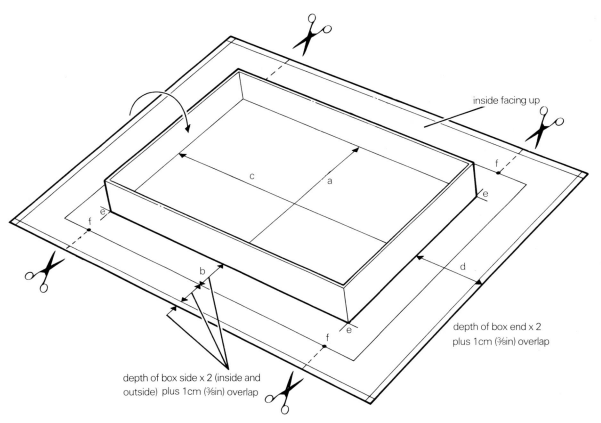

inside facing up

c

a

f

e

e

f

d

depth of box end x 2
plus 1cm (⅜in) overlap

b

e

f

depth of box side x 2 (inside and
outside) plus 1cm (⅜in) overlap

41 *The Cover-up box. Accuracy when calculating the measurements is very important.*

the overlap (fig. 41d). Keep a note of the measurements as it is very important to cut the paper out accurately.

Place the paper, inside facing up, onto a flat surface. Now refer back to your measurements for the depth of the side of the box doubled plus the overlap and, starting at the top left of the paper mark a dot this width in from the edge of the sheet. (In the example given above, this would be 11 cm (4⅜ in).) Mark a second dot the same width in from the bottom left edge of the sheet. Rule a line between the two dots. Repeat on the other side. Repeat this process at both ends of the paper (fig. 41e).

Cover the outside of the lid of the box with adhesive and fix it in place within the ruled lines on the paper. Press firmly on the lid.

Stand the lid on its side with the inside facing you. Making sure the paper is taut, and keeping the lid on its side, rule a line from the edge of the paper to the corner at either end of the box (the line should equal the length of the outside of that side of the box, plus the overlap) (fig. 41f). Cut along these lines (see where the dotted lines end on the diagram). Repeat on the opposite side of the box. Now the paper can be folded inside the lid (fig.

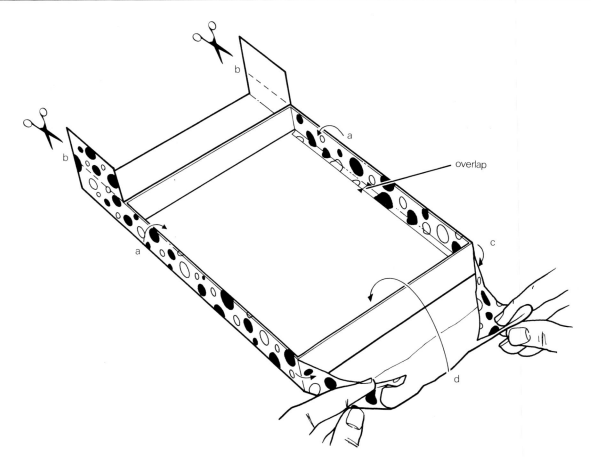

42 Covering the box lid with paper

42a). Using liquid adhesive seal the sides in place, being careful to glue right to the edges of the paper and to keep the paper taut.

Turn one end of the box towards you. Cut off the excess paper at each corner to the height of the box (fig. 42b). With your first fingers, make an inverted triangular pleat at each corner (fig. 42c). Hold the pleats in position with the front of the fingers. Pull up the ends of the paper towards the box — between the pads of your first fingers and thumbs — and roll the edges until they are the exact width of the end of the box (fig. 42d). Don't panic at this point — it is not difficult!

Fold the paper inside the lid. Crease it. Unfold and seal it in place using liquid or stick adhesive.

Repeat steps b, c and d at the other end of the box.

Cut a piece of paper large enough to line the base of the lid of the box. Seal it in place with adhesive.

Repeat the entire process for the bottom of the box.

Whether it's a present for posting, packing, or perhaps a problem shape – a Cover-up's the answer.

6 IT'S A PROBLEM

This chapter deals with some of the problems you might face when gift-wrapping, such as a lack of paper, nothing to decorate your present with, wrapping enormous presents, and how to overcome wrapping awkward shapes. The information given here will help you to become a gift-wrapping 'Houdini'.

LACK OF PAPER

Example 1 You don't have sufficient paper – either on a roll or even a sheet – to wrap around a large gift. No matter. Use more than one sheet of matching or co-ordinating gift-wrap. Carefully line up the sheets, inside face up, and seal them together by running a strip of invisible tape along the join.

Example 2 You thought that sheet of blue paper with the white dots was large enough to wrap your present. It isn't! With some clever mixing and matching this sort of problem can be overcome. Try joining a set of pleats using paper with the same pattern but a different colour combination for a striking effect. In this instance use a sheet of white paper with blue dots. Another way around the problem is to mix patterns of the same colour, for example dots and squares.

Example 3 The news is getting worse – now you find you've run out of wrapping paper altogether. What are the alternatives? There are a few. Cellophane or acetate, patterned or plain, may be able to keep you from the clutches of disaster. Or what about a sheet of scented drawer lining paper, which will make the present smell nice too. Or, if the gift is a bit 'naughty', a plain brown paper wrapping might be most appropriate! If you're wrapping a present for your boss, how about using a page from the *Financial Times* or some other relevant publication – a comic maybe?

Graph paper is another possibility, if you feel like being creative. You can convey your message clearly too. For example, draw a repeat pattern of a chart showing a soaring, upward curve, and write underneath something along the lines of 'This is how much I love you'.

Finally how about a sheet of plain paper on which you can draw your own personalized design (see page 69).

DECORATING WITHOUT RIBBON

If you discover that you have no ribbon to decorate your wrapped gift, do not despair. Here are some suggestions to help you ensure your present is well-dressed.

Example 1 Using some leftover matching or co-ordinating wrapping paper, make a pleated paper bow. This type of bow is ideal for a present that has to be posted or packed in a bag as it lies flat on the present. Dramatic results can be achieved by using paper patterned with diagonal lines.

You need: paper; invisible tape; double-sided tape; scissors; pencil.

Make lengthwise pleats across the full width of the paper. (How much paper you use will depend on how large you want to make the bow.) Seal the pleats in place with invisible tape on the 'inside' of the paper – be generous so that they are all held in place. Now mark the design on the same side of the paper and cut it out (fig. 43a). Fix the bow on the gift using double-sided tape.

Example 2 A gift wrapped in plain paper can look very smart just by adding the initials of the recipient to it. Either use transfers, or cut out large glossy letters from a magazine and stick them to the present.

Example 3 A length of real ribbon tied around a small bunch of fresh or dried flowers can make a lovely decoration on a gift.

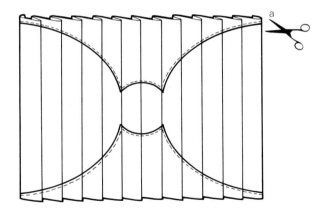

43 No ribbon? No panic! Make this striking pleated paper bow with some leftover gift-wrapping paper.

HOW TO WRAP ENORMOUS PRESENTS

If somebody is lucky enough to be getting a car or washing machine from you, it may be impractical to wrap these gifts! Instead wrap the car keys, together with directions on where to find the car, in a small box; and, so they don't mistake the gleaming silver sports car for the slightly-battered secondhand Ford Escort behind it,

decorate your gift with helium-filled balloons! For the washing machine, wrap something associated with the present, such as a packet of washing powder, together with a note advising him or her of the delivery date; but do put the box in a plastic bag first to stop the smell coming through the wrapping. But if your problem is a little more down-to-earth – wrapping a large, heavy, box for example, remember it's easiest to use a roll of paper rather than joining lots of sheets together. Don't try to wrap the underside which nobody will see. Just tuck the paper underneath the box and seal it with invisible tape.

AWKWARD-SHAPED GIFTS

Now, having looked at various ways to alleviate some of the problems you might encounter, let's tackle some of those you can't avoid – awkward shapes.

Cylindrical bottle

You need: paper (neither very glossy nor very thick to avoid 'veining', but a paper that is densely patterned will hide the creases!); scissors/pinking shears; invisible or clear tape; double-sided tape; ribbon to decorate.

With paper inside face up, roll it around the bottle to see how much you need. Allow extra paper above the top of the bottle (about a quarter), plus extra at one side if you want to make pleats, and at the other to turn over for a neat edge. At the base of the bottle measure paper from the edge inwards to just over half the diameter (fig. 44a). This will enable you to make small, neat overlapping folds.

Cut out the required amount of paper. With the paper still inside face up, fold over one side to ensure a neat edge (fig. 44b). Make pleats along the other side and seal them on the inside with invisible tape (fig. 44c). Run a length of double-sided tape along the pleated or outside edge of the paper where it comes in contact with the cylindrical part of the bottle (fig. 44d). Remove the

All dressed up and ready to go! A selection of bottles wrapped for the party.

backing strip. Place the bottle on the paper in line with the folded inside edge (fig. 44e). Hold the edge of the paper against the bottle and roll the bottle along the paper, making sure it is aligned with the edge of the sheet (fig. 44f). Making sure the paper is taut, roll the bottle over the double-sided tape. Consider the pleated length as the front of the wrapping.

Turn the bottle onto its front and face the end of it towards you (fig. 45). Gradually, starting from the top, then one side, then the other and finally the bottom, work the paper into small folds overlapping each other in a circular shape (fig. 45a). If necessary hold some of the folds in place using double-sided tape. Lift the end of the pleated strip last. Fold over its tip and seal it with double-

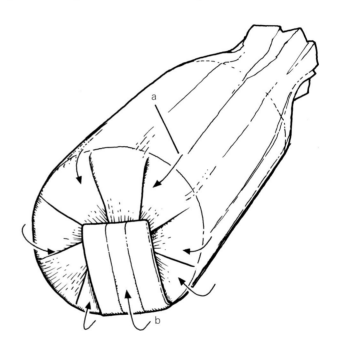

45 Work the paper into small overlapping folds at the base. Pull up the end of the pleated strip last, fold over its tip and seal to the base.

sided tape to the base of the bottle (fig. 45b). If that's too difficult, seal it to the base using clear or invisible tape. Stand the bottle on its end to press the tape firmly in place.

Cut a strip of ribbon long enough to tie around the neck of the bottle. With the front of the bottle facing you,

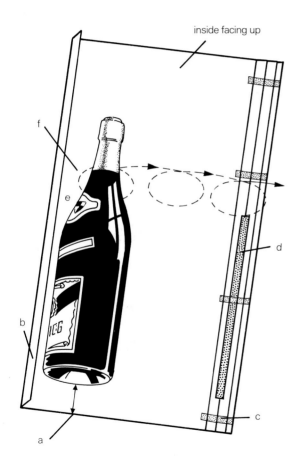

44 Wrapping a cylindrical bottle

gather the paper round the neck by placing your two first fingers to meet at the back, and the tip of your thumbs at the front. Press the paper in at each side with your middle fingers (fig. 46a). Then draw up the inverted pleat to the top of the paper with your thumb and first finger on each hand (fig. 46b). Keep the paper in place at the base of the bottle neck with the thumb and first

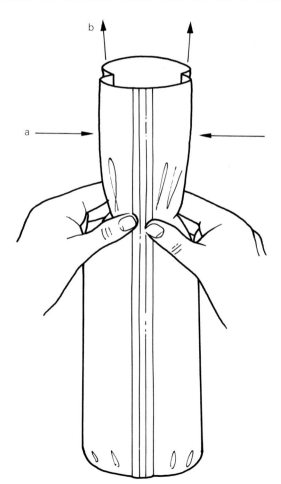

46 *Gathering the paper at the neck of the bottle*

finger of one hand and tie the length of ribbon in place at that point.

At the top of the bottle fold the paper away from you twice. Then make one fold towards you so you have a horizontal pleat across the top of the gift-wrapping. Seal it in place with double-sided tape. You'll need two strips – one behind the pleat to keep it flat and one to hold the pleat against the wrapping.

Alternatively, seal the paper with a strip of double-sided tape fixed horizontally between the back and front of the top of the paper (you may need an extra strip to seal the pleated front in place), and trim the top to whatever shape you prefer, perhaps using pinking shears. Decorate the bottle by adding a bow around the neck.

Curved bottle
Bottles that are curved rather than cylindrical can pose a bit more of a problem, but this is easily overcome by using a more pliable wrapping material. Crinkle foil is ideal as it is so malleable, but ordinary crêpe paper, which is less expensive, will do just as well. Wrap crêpe paper around the bottle more than once as it is quite see-through and follow the same directions as for wrapping a cylindrical bottle, sealing it at the top with double-sided tape. Do not try to make a horizontal pleat at the top of the bottle, but instead scallop the top edge of the paper with pinking shears.

Square bottle
Cut out the required length of paper allowing approximately a quarter above the top of the bottle and just over half the diameter of the base below the bottle. It needs to be wide enough to wrap around the bottle with extra for a small overlap.

With the paper inside face up, fold over both sides and run a strip of double-sided tape all the way along one

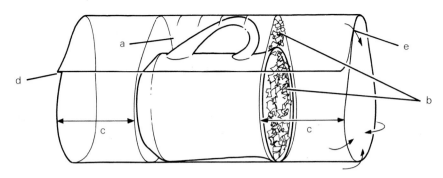

47 Wrapping a mug. A length of card placed around the gift not only makes it easier to wrap but also enables you to keep the contents a mystery.

side. Put the bottle face down on the paper. Position the bottle so that you seal the overlap along one of the four corners. Keep it on its front, with the seal along one of the corners and the base of the bottle facing you, fold the end armchair style (page 16). If the base is not exactly square, fold the paper in gently.

Stand the bottle up and, facing it in front of you, trim the top of the paper if necessary. Then gently, using both middle fingers – invert the paper at each side above the height of the square shoulder of the bottle as you did for a cylindrical bottle (fig. 46). Fold the top of the paper away from you twice and seal it in place with double-sided tape. A large bow-tie (perhaps made out of sequin scrap and satinwrap, page 34) fixed to the sloping top half of the wrapping is particularly effective.

Mug

Wrapping a mug with the handle sticking out is not only difficult to wrap but also easy to guess the contents. Just by wrapping cardboard around it, both these problems can be solved!

You need: length of card; pencil and ruler; scissors; double-sided tape; tissue-paper; wrapping paper (preferably patterned, but not glossy or very thick to avoid 'veining'); invisible tape; ribbon to decorate.

Using a pencil and ruler, measure a strip of card the height of the mug and wide enough to wrap around it (fig. 47a). Cut it out. Holding the card tightly around the mug, seal it in place with double-sided or invisible tape.

Fill the mug with tissue-paper, so you now have a firm top and base (fig. 47b). Cut out enough paper to wrap around the card, allowing extra for two neat edges at the sides, plus approximately half the width of the diameter at the top and bottom of the mug (fig. 47c). Wrap the paper around the card and seal it in place using double-sided tape on the outside edge (fig. 47d). Place the mug on its side with the sealed edge facing up. Turn one end of the mug towards you and starting at the top, and going down the sides, make small overlapping folds (fig. 47e) as for the base of the cylindrical bottle. Make the folds at the bottom last and seal to the base with double-sided or invisible tape. Repeat at the other end.

Stand the mug upright and decorate on top with a full or snip bow (page 32).

Round container

You need: paper; scissors; double-sided tape; invisible tape.

Measure paper wide enough to roll around the circumference of the container allowing a little extra

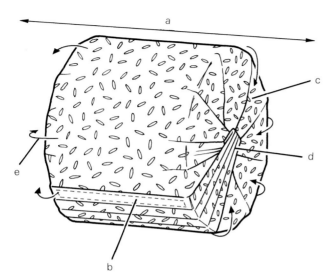

48 *Wrapping a round container*

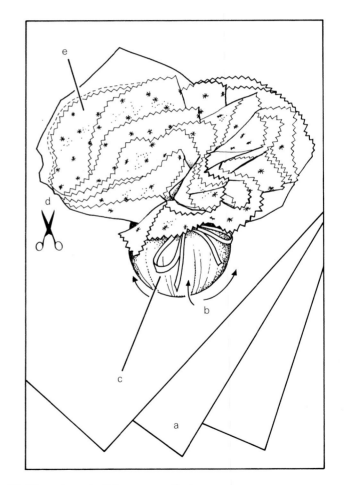

Ball

You need: crêpe paper; scissors; ribbon; stick or liquid adhesive; glitter or other decoration; sheet of newspaper.

Cut enough squares of paper so that you can't see the gift through the paper when it is wrapped (fig. 49a). The size of these squares will depend on the size of the ball. Allow sufficient to be able to pull the paper up over the

either side for two neat edges, or the inside edge and the pleated front. In these instructions the gift is wrapped with pleats. The length of the paper should be the height of the box plus just over half the diameter of the top and base at each side (fig. 48a).

With the paper inside face up, fold over the inside edge and make lengthwise pleats along the outside edge. Seal them in place with invisible tape. Run a strip of double-sided tape along the pleated or outside edge. Remove the backing strip. Put the container on its side and, starting from the inside edge, roll the paper around it and seal with the tape (fig. 48b). With the pleated front face down and one end of the container facing you, start to fold the paper from the top and down each side in small overlapping folds (fig. 48c). Fold up the pleated section last. Turn over its tip and seal with double-sided tape (fig. 48d).

Repeat this folding process on the other end (fig. 48e). Decorate on top with a full bow or a snip bow (page 32).

49 *Wrapping a ball in squares of crêpe paper*

A wedding day collection: iris film covers a basket, and the twin packs are mugs in disguise.

gift easily and tie on top with extra to spare. Cut a length of ribbon.

Put the squares together, each at a slight angle. Place the ball on top. Gather up the crêpe paper by first joining the opposite corners and then clasping all the paper tightly on top of the ball (fig. 49b). Tie in position with the ribbon and make a bow (fig. 49c).

Place the wrapped gift on a sheet of newspaper and trim the top into a rounded shape using pinking shears (fig. 49d). Separate the sheets to give a tufted or layered appearance, like a ballerina's tutu. Dab the tufted top with adhesive and then sprinkle with glitter, stars or other decorative shapes (fig. 49e). Shake off the excess and leave to dry. Pour the leftover glitter back into the container.

An ornament

When you are buying an ornament that doesn't come in its own box, it is worth asking the shop assistant if they have a spare box you could have. Alternatively, wrap it in a Cover-up (page 43). In this case it should be wrapped in tissue-paper or bubble wrap, and then if necessary held secure in the box with scrunched up tissue-paper or polystyrene chips.

Another idea is to wrap it in tissue-paper and cellophane. This is only practical if you will be able to transport the present easily without risk of getting it broken.

For the cellophane wrap you need: tissue-paper in a colour of your choice; cellophane (perhaps patterned); scissors or pinking shears; ribbon.

Cut out enough cellophane and tissue-paper (you might need more than one sheet) to cover the gift with extra to spare.

Lay the cellophane on a flat surface with the sheet of tissue-paper on top of it. Place the gift in the middle and, starting with the corners, gather the cellophane and

tissue-paper tightly into a central point above it. Secure by tying a strip of ribbon in a knot (this will prevent the gift from rolling around). Trim the top of the tissue-paper and cellophane using scissors or pinking shears.

Add a bow or other decoration to the ribbon. If you have cut the cellophane with pinking shears, see what spectacular results you get by cutting the ribbon in the same way.

Clothing

Items of clothing all have something in common – their soft and squashy shape, and this means you often end up with an equally squashed wrap! A simple way to overcome this problem is to place a firm sheet of cardboard on your gift which will act as a base when you seal down the paper.

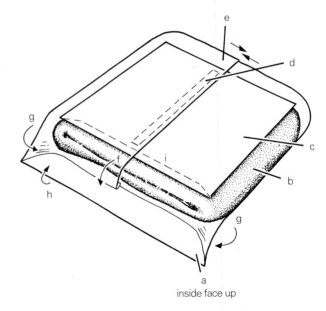

inside face up

50 *A sheet of cardboard placed on top of the clothing gives a firm base on which to seal the paper*

You need: sheet of firm cardboard; wrapping paper; tissue-paper; scissors; double-sided tape; ribbon to decorate.

Fold the garment neatly and wrap it in tissue-paper. If the card is a bit tatty, cover it in paper too. Work out how much paper you need by loosely wrapping the gift and card and allowing a little extra each side for an overlap. Now cut the paper out.

With the paper inside face up (fig. 50a), place the gift on it (fig. 50b) with the card on top (fig. 50c). Fold over both sides of the paper for neat edges and run a strip of double-sided tape along the full length of one of the sides (fig. 50d). Remove the backing strip. Ensure the paper is not too loosely wrapped around the gift and overlap the two edges of paper (fig. 50e).

Turn one end towards you. Fold down the top flap (fig. 50f). Then fold in the two sides (fig. 50g). Fold up the base and turn in the tip of the paper to give a neat edge (fig. 50h). Seal it to the firm 'base' on top (fig. 50i).

Turn the package right side up and decorate.

Socks or other unexciting items

Crackers don't just need to be for Christmas. They are a way of making a gift that is not very exciting, like a pair of socks, a bit more fun. Don't use thick or very glossy paper which will mark easily; it is better to use thinner paper or crêpe or tissue-paper.

You need: cardboard; wrapping paper; tissue-paper; scissors or pinking shears; double-sided tape; ribbon strips and ribbon to decorate.

Roll the gift into a sausage shape. Wrap it loosely in tissue-paper. Cut a piece of card long enough to make a cylinder around the 'sausage' (fig. 51a). Seal it using double-sided tape.

Measure wrapping paper four times the length of the cylinder (to allow for trimming of the ends) and wide enough to seal around it with a small overlap. Allow extra in the width if you want to pleat the paper. Cut out the amount required.

Fold over one side and pleat the other side (or just fold it over), and run a strip of double-sided tape along the

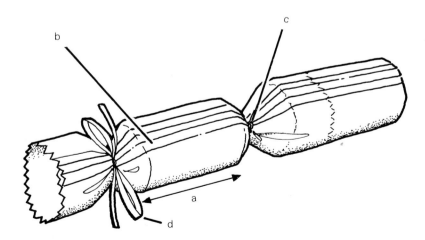

51 *Crackers don't just have to be for Christmas. They can make an interesting wrap for a pair of socks, for example.*

inside of the pleated (or outside) edge. Remove the backing strip. Roll the paper around the cylinder and seal it. The pleats (if you have any) are now the 'front' of the present (fig. 51b).

Carefully clasp the paper at each end of the cylinder and hold in place with a strip of ribbon (fig. 51c). Trim the ends of the paper and add a bow or other decoration to the ribbon at each end (fig. 51d).

Cosmetics

Here is a speedy and inexpensive way to package an assortment of cosmetic items — the pots of colour, the blusher, mascara and lipstick — all in one neat wrap. Use a plastic tray such as those often found under pre-packed supermarket produce. Make sure it is large enough to hold all the items you wish to wrap. Wash and dry the tray.

You need: plastic tray; tissue-paper; cling film; clear tape; scissors; ribbon to decorate.

Place the tray in the centre of the sheet of tissue-paper. Fold the paper over into the tray and scrunch up the excess to make a bed on which to place the gifts. When you like your arrangement of the cosmetics, cover the basket with cling film and seal it underneath with clear tape. Decorate the top with ribbon and a bow.

Cooking utensils

This collection makes an ideal gift for someone moving into their first home; it is also a novel present for an engagement party. Use a cylindrical container. Buy one to co-ordinate with the colour scheme in the kitchen, or cover a wide-necked bottle with wrapping paper. Make sure the container is wide enough at the neck to hold the utensils.

You need: wide-necked bottle; paper; scissors; double-sided tape; an elastic band; stapler; ribbon to decorate.

Cover the bottle following the directions on page 49 except on this occasion just fold the paper into the top of the jar. Arrange the gifts standing inside the jar and cover with clear cellophane. Gather the cellophane at the neck of the bottle (or just below the top of the container) and hold it in place with an elastic band. Trim off the excess cellophane and tie a ribbon over the elastic band. Make the ribbon into a bow.

Flowers and pot plants

These, together with the box of chocolates, must be the most frequently-given present — an emergency stand-by for all sorts of occasions. Dress up home-grown or shop-bought flowers with an original cellophane 'wrap'.

For a bouquet you need: cellophane; scissors; ribbon.

Build up an arrangement of flowers into a round shape, while holding them in one hand. Wrap the cellophane in place by tying ribbon around the stems. Trim any excess cellophane and add a bow to the wrapping.

For a pot plant you need: cellophane; ribbon; scissors; clear tape.

Cut cellophane measuring more than double the height of the plant plus the pot, and greater than its width so that the plant will be completely covered. Fold the cellophane in half over the plant and hold it in place just below the top of the flower pot. Fold over the sides and seal them in place with clear tape. Tie a strip of ribbon around the pot tightly and fix it in position with clear tape. Finally seal the excess cellophane underneath the pot with clear tape.

To decorate the wrapping, tie a bow to the ribbon at the front of the pot.

Triangular box

You need: paper; scissors; double-sided tape; ribbon to decorate.

It's a blooming good idea to wrap gifts of plants or flowers in cellophane.

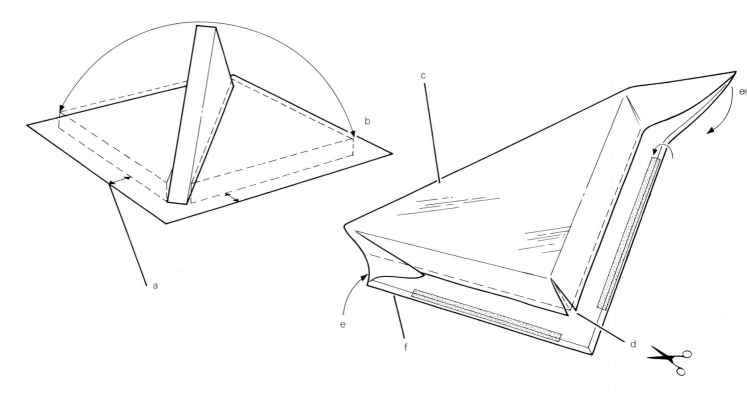

52 *A triangular box.* **Left** *Measuring out the paper.* **Right** *Wrapping the gift.*

Place the triangle in one corner of a sheet of paper, allowing for a border of paper equalling the depth of the box (fig. 52a). Carefully stand the box up, and then lay it down on the opposite side (fig. 52b). Again allow extra for the depth of the box, and cut the paper out.

Place the box on the paper in its original position (fig. 52a). Fold the paper over the triangle (fig. 52c). Snip the top point of the paper to the box to make two flaps and fold them down against the side of the box (fig. 52d). Seal the overlapping tips with double-sided tape. Fold the 'wings' of paper in place at either end of the box (fig. 52e). With one side of the box facing you, fold over

the outside edge of the paper for neatness (fig. 52f), and seal in place against the side of the box with double-sided tape. Repeat on the other side of the box. Decorate the wrapped gift with a bow.

Hexagonal box
You need: paper; scissors; double-sided tape; stapler; ribbon to decorate.

Wrap the paper around the box to gauge how much you need. Allow half the depth of the box at each end. Cut out the required paper.

With the paper inside face up fold over both edges and

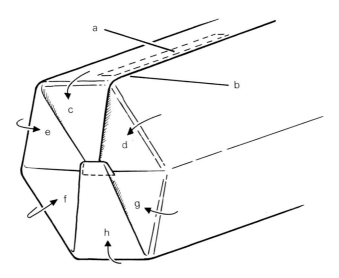

53 *Wrapping an hexagonal box*

fix a strip of double-sided tape along one of the edges (fig. 53a). Remove the backing strip. Carefully overlap the two edges and seal in place (fig. 53b).

At one end, fold the top of the paper in making triangular folds towards the centre of the box – but don't crease the lines (fig. 53c). Then pull the segments on either side of it (d and e) towards the centre; then f and g. Pull up the last segment (h) and crease it into a triangular shape. Fold over the tip of the paper and seal it in place with double-sided tape.

Repeat at the other end. Decorate with a full or snip bow on top. If you prefer to make the box into a 'cracker', seal a full bow at each end so that it lies on one side.

7 HOME IS WHERE THE ART IS!

Growing or making the gifts you give can be very satisfying, and, for the recipient, it is equally gratifying to receive a gift that has been specially produced for them. If you go to this trouble, you certainly want your results to look their best. Making a pound of tomatoes from the hothouse or a pot of preserve look exciting is not as difficult as it might at first seem. In this chapter you will delight at the difference a doily can make, or how those fruit and vegetable trays you get from the supermarket or greengrocer can be put to good use instead of filling your bin. And wait till you see the creative cocoons you can make with cellophane!

HOME-MADE CONFECTIONERY
It's a real show-stopper at the end of a dinner party to serve home-made *petit fours* or truffles with coffee. Or how about making some to take to someone else's party instead of the predictable bunch of flowers or bottle of wine? They also make wonderful Christmas presents or can help to cheer up a chum who is feeling a little glum.

Petit fours or chocolate truffles
It's best to display these delicacies on a firm base to prevent them getting crushed. At last you can put all those 'odd' saucers in the cupboard to good use, or look out for antique bargains on market stalls. Alternatively, use a party plate in paper or plastic.

You need: a saucer or some other dish; doily; cling film; clear tape; ribbon to decorate; scissors.

Place a doily on the dish – a gold one adds a festive touch – and then arrange the sweets on it. Cover the dish tightly with cling film to keep them fresh and also to stop them from rolling about. Carefully seal the cling film to the saucer using clear tape. Decorate your gift with a bow (see pages 28–34).

Alternatively, substitute the cling film for cellophane. Cut out a square of cellophane large enough to place the saucer in the middle and have extra to gather in a tuft above the sweets. Use pinking shears to give an attractive edging.

Having arranged the sweets on a doily in the dish, place it in the centre of the sheet of cellophane. (For a seasonal touch at Christmas use snow-patterned acetate.) Gather the cellophane above the centre of the dish and clasp it in a ring just above the truffles or *petit fours* to prevent them from moving about. Tie a length of ribbon tightly around the base of the tuft and add a bow to the ribbon.

Turkish delight or fingers of fudge
As they are less likely to crumble, pieces of Turkish delight or fudge need not be wrapped on a firm base. You can simply place them on a square of cellophane. If necessary, use a doily to separate layers. If the Turkish delight is in two colours, try arranging it in a chequerboard design.

You need: cellophane; doily; ribbon; scissors.

Gently gather the cellophane tightly on top of the Turkish delight or fudge and tie with a ribbon. Decorate with a bow.

FRUIT AND VEGETABLES

Using this same method with cellophane you can make home-grown fruit or vegetables look extra appetizing. Try it for instance with plums, cherries, gooseberries, tomatoes, or even trimmed radishes.

If you are taking a bunch of grapes to a friend who is ill, banish the boring brown paper bag. Try wrapping them instead in cellophane and decorate with a ribbon. Just what the doctor ordered! Or how about a garland of fruit? (I do not recommend you to try this with melons!)

A fruit garland

You need: six round pieces of fruit (small but firm, for example satsumas); crêpe paper; scissors; thin strips of ribbon.

Place the pieces of fruit in a line. Measure a length of crêpe paper approximately twice their total length (fig. 54a). The paper needs to be wide enough to wrap around the fruit twice (or one-and-a-half times for some

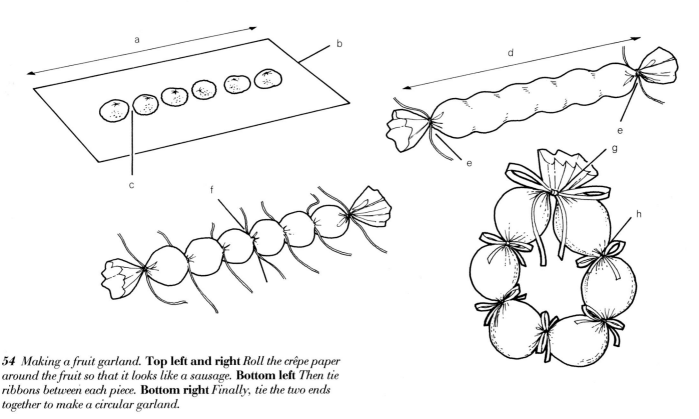

54 *Making a fruit garland.* **Top left and right** *Roll the crêpe paper around the fruit so that it looks like a sausage.* **Bottom left** *Then tie ribbons between each piece.* **Bottom right** *Finally, tie the two ends together to make a circular garland.*

interesting shading) (fig. 54b). Cut out.

Spread the fruit along the length of the paper, leaving space between each one and paper at each end (fig. 54c). Roll the paper around the fruit (so that it begins to look like a long sausage) (fig. 54d).

Cut out narrow strips of ribbon to tie between each of the pieces. Carefully start tying at each end (fig. 54e) – knotting the ribbon tightly – and work towards the middle of the sausage. When you have tied all the ribbons your sausage should have been replaced with a centipede (fig. 54f)!

Tie the two ends together to make a circular garland (fig. 54g). Either trim all the ribbons or, better still, make them into little bows (fig. 54h).

JAMS, PRESERVES, PICKLES AND CHUTNEY

Jars of home-made jam, preserve, pickles and chutney all make very tasty gifts. After all your labours, let's look at some simple finishing touches.

You need: sticky labels; felt-tip pens and metallic markers; crêpe paper; crinkle foil or cellophane; double-sided or clear tape; scissors.

First of all, the label. Use sticky labels, but instead of just indicating the contents and the date, give an extra hint by sticking a picture of the fruit or vegetable on it. You can cut it out of a magazine or, if you are really feeling creative, why not draw it?

To wrap the jar you can use crêpe paper, or other flexible wrapping paper (follow the directions for wrapping a cylindrical bottle on page 49). Or how about something completely different?

Cut clear cellophane to go around the jar with enough to fold underneath and seal, plus extra on top to tie in a tuft. Lie the cellophane flat on a clean surface and cover it in a repeat pattern using a metallic marker (or correction pen for 'White Christmas' messages!) with a

design of your choice (e.g. Gerda's Homemade Jam * Gerda's Homemade Jam * /strawberry * strawberry * strawberry *). When the ink is dry, wrap the jar as directed on page 49. It is safe to use ink here as it doesn't come in contact with the food. However, I do not recommend that you use ink on cellophane that touches food, for example, the Turkish delight.

HOME-MADE WINE

You need: sticky label; cellophane; metallic marker; scissors; clear tape.

Be creative with the label on a bottle of home-made wine. Don't just write the date you bottled it and what wine it is. Draw a vine around the label or something else associated with the contents.

Cut out sufficient cellophane to wrap around the bottle with a small overlap. Allow extra both above the top of the bottle where it will be tied with ribbon, and beneath it where it will be sealed with clear tape. Follow the instructions on page 49 for wrapping a cylindrical bottle, substituting cellophane for the paper and clear tape for double-sided tape.

If you are taking a bottle of wine as a gift for dinner, try writing a message of thanks on the cellophane wrap.

BISCUITS AND CAKES

If you are making biscuits or cakes to sell at a bazaar or to give to friends, you can make them extra appetizing by wrapping them rather than just popping a pile into a plastic bag; and by using a shallow plastic tray, kept from a supermarket purchase of vegetables or fruit, you can ensure that variety is the spice of everybody's life!

You need: shallow plastic tray; doily; cling film; scissors; clear tape; ribbon to decorate.

Clean and dry the tray. Cut a doily to line the inside. Arrange on it a selection of biscuits or a mouth-watering mixture of cake slices.

Cover the tray tightly with cling film and seal it underneath. Decorate on top with ribbon.

POT-POURRI

A pot-pourri is a mixture of dried petals and spices kept for its perfume. It's a wonderful way to preserve flowers from the garden, or a bouquet that holds particular memories – perhaps from your wedding day.

Using home-grown flowers you can also make several types of perfumed presents. Once you've checked which flowers are best to preserve and have carried out the necessary steps to dry them properly, you may like to make some of the gifts below.

Bowl or basket

You need: glass or china bowl, or basket; cling film; clear tape; scissors; ribbon.

Pour some of your mixture of pot-pourri into a bowl or basket, and cover it tightly with cling film. Seal underneath with clear tape. Decorate with ribbon.

Pouch

You need: very fine curtain netting; scissors; needle and thread; velvet or satin ribbon.

Stitch a square of the netting into a pouch shape and pour the pot-pourri inside. Tie up the top of the pouch with a length of velvet or satin ribbon and secure with tacking stitches. If you give this pouch with a present of clothing, it can later be hung on a hanger to keep the garment smelling sweet.

Sachet

You need: very fine curtain netting; scissors; needle and thread; velvet or satin ribbon; Cover-up box; ribbon band.

Sew up a square of the netting leaving one side open. Pour in the pot-pourri and sew up this side. Decorate the sachet with ribbon. A set of sachets in a Cover-up box make an attractive gift, especially handy if it is being posted as they are very lightweight. (For instructions on how to make the box and ribbon band see pages 43–46.)

Decoration

You need: iris film; scissors; velvet or satin ribbon.

Place a small amount of pot-pourri on a double layer of iris film (iridescent cellophane). Gather up the cellophane and clasp it in a ring above the petals. Tie a long length of ribbon around it and make a knot. Attach this to the ribbon decorating a gift and make a bow. Later, the contents can be poured into a dish.

JEWELRY

This is one of the reasons why you've been keeping those empty boxes with separate lids. They make ideal presentation boxes for your handmade jewelry or home-strung beads. On pages 44–46 you will see how to turn the box into a Cover-up.

You need: Cover-up box; ribbon band; wadding (available from fabric departments in most stores).

Choose a box sufficiently large to hold the gift. If you would like it to look like a traditional jewelry box why not cover it in flock paper. Cut out a piece of wadding large enough to fit into the base of the box; and arrange your gift on it. Close the box and decorate with a ribbon band. (For instructions on how to make a cardboard triangle to hang your gift of jewelry on the Christmas tree, see page 74.)

KNITWEAR

A Cover-up box is also ideal when it comes to wrapping knitted goods as they can be a difficult shape to wrap.

You need: Cover-up box; ribbon band; tissue-paper; a sticker seal; scissors.

Feast your eyes on these gift-wrapping ideas for home-made goodies.

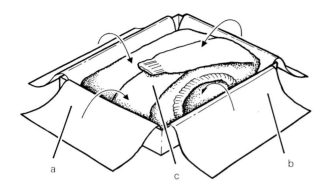

Choose the right size box for the present and wrap it according to the directions on page 44.

Line the box with two sheets of tissue-paper, one lengthways (fig. 55a) and the other widthways (fig. 55b). Place the gift in the box (fig. 55c) and fold each side of tissue over the garment. Seal the tissue with a sticker. Close the box and add a ribbon band.

55 A Cover-up box is ideal for wrapping knitwear. Line the box with tissue paper. Seal the tissue paper with a sticker.

8   IT'S A CELEBRATION

By now you'll have at least wrapped a simple shape, practised pleating paper, or bowled yourself over making beautiful bows, so it probably is a time for a celebration! Now that you have mastered the basic techniques, are you experimenting with different materials and ideas to create new and original wraps or cards? To help you on your way, this chapter concentrates on suggestions for wrapping and decorating gifts for all sorts of occasions rather than giving you very detailed instructions.

BABY PRESENTS

There is a vast selection of wrapping paper designed especially for baby gifts. However, if you can't find one you like, how about choosing a plain colour paper in traditional pink or blue? In the event of twins, a girl and a boy, you could link the decoration on the gifts. Use pink paper with a blue ribbon and blue paper with a pink ribbon.

If you choose patterned paper, this often provides excellent opportunities to make matching gift tags. For example, if the design includes the letters of the alphabet, cut out the baby's initial and stick it to a piece of coloured card or mounting board. All you need to do then is shape the card and punch a hole through it for the ribbon. If the design includes nappy pins, why not tie some real ones to the gift-wrapping ribbon?

Soft toys can be a problem to wrap because they are such an awkward shape, with arms, legs and paws all over the place. Clear cellophane can be the answer to this problem. Tie a bow around the animal's neck. Wrap the toy in cellophane and seal it in place using clear tape. Decorate the wrapping with more ribbon in a matching colour.

You'll find lots of ideas for making gift tags and cards on pages 35–42. Instead of sending a card to the parents, how about making a personalized card for the baby? Choose the size of card you want and fold it in half. Rule a border around the edge using a felt-tip pen. On the front write the baby's name using the same colour ink with perhaps gold or silver 'freckles' on top (dot each letter with a metallic marker to get this effect).

To decorate the gift, tie a small gift, like a rattle, to the bow, but make sure it is sterilized before being given to the baby.

CHILDREN'S BIRTHDAYS

When it comes to choosing the paper, look out for sheets printed with the child's name, age or favourite television or story-book character. Here again you can turn a leftover scrap of paper into a gift tag or card (see pages 35–42).

Decorate the wrapping using ribbon with a 'Happy Birthday' message printed on it. Or, pin a name or age badge to the gift tag or card.

A Cover-up gets over the problem of wrapping a difficult shape (pages 43–47). By using flock paper in different colours you can transform even the tattiest box into a treasure chest. Design a picture on top or add a personal touch by spelling the child's name on the lid.

If the child likes to play 'pass the parcel', wrap his or her present in several layers of paper. You can use up creased paper below the surface wrapping as he or she will, no doubt, be more interested in shedding the layers than admiring your handiwork! Or using the same idea, replace the paper for boxes of ever-increasing size. Put the gift in the smallest and while gift-wrapping only the largest box, tie ribbon around each of the boxes.

A PERSONALIZED WRAP

The ultimate designer paper can be a big hit on any occasion! Specially personalized for parents, grand-parents, aunts and uncles, it can be made on a rainy afternoon and kept until the 'day'. Make sure you use pens, paint or ink that won't smudge. The paper can also be decorated with glitter or paper shapes, but remember to work on a sheet of newspaper to avoid an unexpected spot of spring cleaning! Don't make the design too spacious, otherwise when the paper is folded the pattern won't show up. A close repeat pattern works well.

Personalized paper can be designed to suit all occasions. Here are some ideas to start you off.

Happy Birthday Mum Write a continuous line of the greeting. Underneath it add a line of hugs and kisses (OXOXOXO). Repeat this pattern to the end of the paper. You can vary the size of the letters according to the size of the gift.

Love You Grandpa Using two or more colours and lettering in different styles and sizes, write your message randomly across the paper and punctuate each time with a heart shape. This dizzy pattern makes it easier to wrap awkward-shaped gifts as it covers up the creases!

You are Number 1 Punctuate your message with paper shapes, like gold stars.

56 A design for a silver wedding anniversary wrapping paper

Silver Wedding Anniversary Using a silver metallic marker write the number 25 at intervals across the paper. Write your message in a continuous repeat pattern between the curves.

Merry Christmas Carine For personalized Christmas paper, choose your message and write it in block letters in a repeat pattern across the paper. Turn the paper upside down and write the message in script along the in-between lines. You could also write the message in alternating colours to make it stand out. You will be able to read the greeting whichever way round you hold the present.

Take a bow, and some ribbons, for a Happy Birthday celebration.

LOVE AND STUFF

When it comes to wrapping presents for special occasions including engagements, weddings and anniversaries or St Valentine's Day, there is a plethora of paper to choose from, particularly a wide range of heart designs which will often rescue you when making last-minute wraps!

How about adding an extra 'layer' to your wrapping to throw the recipient off the scent altogether? My mother got quite a surprise when, on the morning of their twenty-fifth wedding anniversary, all my father presented her with was a cased bar of soap – or so she thought! On opening it, she discovered a beautiful brooch inside.

As always, see if you can use some of the leftover wrapping paper when making tags, especially if you can incorporate a message printed on it, for example, 'Congratulations!'. And, perhaps, cut the tag in a heart shape.

When decorating your present try mixing plain coloured ribbon with one patterned with wedding bells or some other appropriate design.

On the subject of anniversaries, did you know that several are represented by different symbols? Not just gold, silver and diamond either! Not only can you give a gift of the symbol, for example a leather purse or wallet, or a silk tie or pyjamas, but you can also incorporate the symbol into the wrapping and the card or gift tag.

Leather Three years. 'Wrap' the gift in a leather pouch. This is especially appropriate if you are giving jewelry as the present. The gift tag can be a leather luggage label!

Silk Four years. Decorate your gift with silk flowers. You can also use a thin length of silk ribbon to tie through your gift tag. Remember to make reference in the wording to it being a silk anniversary.

Wood Five years. If you are a DIY enthusiast you can have some fun by making a wooden box to 'wrap' the gift in. Or use an empty cigar or orange box. The wording on the tag could read 'Wood'en you know it's your fifth anniversary!'

Lace Thirteen years. Wrap your gift with lace-patterned paper or ribbon. If you use a shoe-lace to tie the tag to a gift make sure you explain your reason in the wording!

Silver Twenty-five years. There's a multitude of metallic PVC or foil papers and ribbon to choose from. Try adding a hint of another colour to intensify the effect of the silver. On your card or tag, write with a silver metallic marker or decorate it with silver glitter.

Pearl Thirty years. Use pearlized paper or iridescent cellophane, like iris film, for a 'mother of pearl' look. Or, make a Cover-up box and decorate the lid with pearls. A broken string of cheap pearls (as against those handed down from your great-great grandmother!), entwined with ribbon, can create entrancing results when it comes to decorating the wrapping.

Gold Fifty years. Try adding a gold patterned cellophane or acetate overlay on gold paper. Perhaps cover the ribbon with a strip of the overlay too for a really glamorous gift. Use a gold metallic marker or glitter when making your card or tag.

Diamond Sixty years. A chance to really 'go to town' by using either diamond-patterned diffraction foil or, if you prefer, a plain paper wrap, and add a diamanté earring (broken of course!) to the ribbon or bow for a truly sparkling touch!

MOTHER'S/FATHER'S DAY

If you give more than a card on this day, how about having some fun with the gift tag?

Design one to look like a voucher entitling one breakfast in bed, one free washing up, one bunch of flowers on request, one car wash, one shoe cleaning, or whatever is most appropriate.

HOUSE-WARMING GIFTS

When it comes to wrapping a house-warming present, wallpaper could be a subtle hint if there is a lot of redecorating to be done! Make a matching tag with wording along the lines of 'Welcome to your New Home. Don't say we didn't help with the decorating!'

If you choose a more conventional gift-wrapping, how about making a tag to look like the house? Instead of folding a piece of card exactly in half, make the front half shorter than the back. The short side is the roof (fig. 57a) and covered in sequin scrap it looks tiled! Below the roof, on the inside of the back half of the tag draw or dot in the windows or door (fig. 57b). Lift the roof flap and write your message inside, for example 'Happy Days in your New Home'.

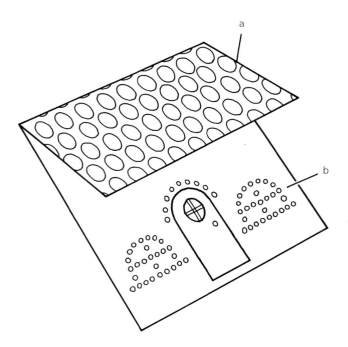

57 A gift tag for a house-warming present

When wrapping the gift have you thought of adding a hint about the contents. How about tying the 'hint' to the ribbon? One of my friends, Simon, likes the Chinese dish, Peking duck. I gave him a poster which showed the eyes and mouth of a duck at the top and his feet at the bottom, with the words 'Peeking Duck' printed in the middle. I wrapped the present with a pair of chopsticks through the ribbons!

PRESENTATIONS AT WORK

Gifts for work colleagues can be wrapped in the pages of a relevant magazine or newspaper, for example a page from a financial or trade journal.

When a presentation is to be made at a retirement party use a sheet of cellophane (plain or patterned) to wrap the present. That way you don't have to worry if it is an awkward shape and it also means that those who contributed to the gift can see what has been given. Decorate the gift with a smart bow.

CHRISTMAS

Apart from choosing from a wide range of printed Christmas paper and ribbon you could also think about more traditional wrapping. Wrap all the men's gifts in green paper with red velvet ribbon and all the women's in red paper with green velvet ribbon. Matching tags of course!

Christmas time seems to bring many gift-wrappers out of hibernation and into a panic about the number of gifts they must wrap! If you want to plan ahead, save boxes during the year and use Christmas paper to turn them into seasonal Cover-ups – the ideal solution for awkward-shaped gifts made up of many parts and those inevitable last-minute purchases (pages 43–47).

Handmade tags and cards, not to mention matching envelopes in all shapes and sizes, can be made well in advance. Some ideas are included in Tagging along, pages 35–42. Another suggestion is to cut out a tree-shape on green card. Outline the edges with metallic ink and decorate with stars or glitter stuck on with adhesive. The tub at its base can be made out of an off-cut of ribbon. Alternatively fold a piece of card in half and draw a tree on the front. Use small shapes of wrapping paper to represent presents around the base of the tree. Seal them with adhesive. Write your message inside the card.

A Christmas cracker

Christmas wouldn't be the same without crackers – so how about making some of your own? We've already seen on page 57 that crackers can disguise a gift or take the problem out of packaging peculiar shapes; they can also be used on the Christmas table to create a novel seating plan by just fixing a small place card to the front of each cracker.

Save the rolls from toilet paper, cling film or kitchen paper. You can also use up odds and ends of paper and patterned cellophane or acetate when it comes to decorating the crackers.

You need: tissue-paper; paper (crêpe paper or crinkle foil guarantee good results); cardboard roll; double-sided tape; scissors/pinking shears; stick or liquid adhesive; ribbon. Optional: snap strips carefully removed with party hats and jokes from an inexpensive box of crackers.

Take a cardboard roll and a small gift which will fit inside it. Wrap the gift loosely in tissue, perhaps with a paper hat and joke. Pull the snap through the roll and secure it with tape at one end. Then put the wrapped gift inside the roll.

Using pinking shears cut the paper allowing for three and a half times the length of the roll and wide enough to wrap around it twice (fig. 58a). Place the roll in the middle of the paper. Wrap the paper firmly around the roll. Secure it in place with double-sided tape. This seam is now the back of the cracker.

Cut paper in another colour, again with pinking

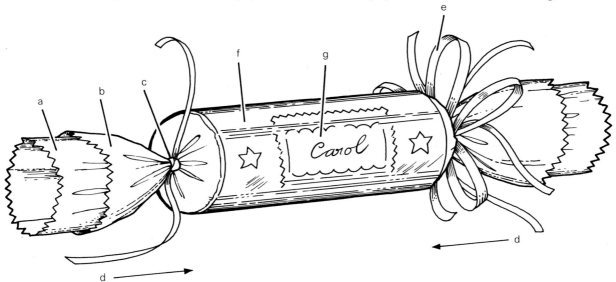

58 Making a Christmas cracker

shears, but this time allow double the length of the roll and enough to wrap around it once. Secure it in place using double-sided tape at the back (fig. 58b).

Gather the paper at each end of the roll and secure tightly with a thin strip of red ribbon (fig. 58c). Gently push the knots towards the barrel of the cracker to improve the shape (fig. 58d). Using pinking shears once again, cut two wider lengths of ribbon approximately 50 cm (19⅝ in). Tie them around each knot and make a bow (fig. 58e). Trim the excess.

To decorate the barrel, wrap a strip of patterned cellophane or acetate around it (fig. 58f). Seal at the back. Make a name card and decorate it (fig. 58g). Using double-sided tape, fix the name card to the front of the cracker. Open out the ends of the cracker slightly using the first three fingers of one hand to complete the cracker shape.

Food Hampers

At Christmas time hampers of food make excellent presents. Not only can you have a lot of fun deciding on the contents but they also make an ideal present for someone who may not be able to afford some of the more expensive edible extras.

You can buy the food gradually (but check the 'sell-by' date). For someone with limited means, choose a balance between practical and luxury items.

How about including some home-made goodies? Maybe a bottle of wine, some preserves or pickles, a plate of *petit fours* (see pages 62–65).

The hamper can be any size, from a bread basket (for a few items), to a bicycle or picnic basket (watch out for bargains on market stalls). You could also make one out of cardboard or a wooden orange box.

For the cardboard hamper you need: a box; wrapping paper and/or tissue-paper; cellophane; scissors; invisible or clear tape; ribbon to decorate.

Cover the box, both inside and out with wrapping paper. Line it with scrunched up or shredded paper.

Arrange the gifts on the bedding. Cut out cellophane large enough to cover the top and sides of the hamper. Tuck it inside the edges of the box. Decorate the hamper with ribbon and a big bow.

Tree triangles

Not only are they a fun way to 'wrap' small gifts, but they also double as dazzling decor on the Christmas tree (but be very careful as they are highly inflammable: definitely don't hang tree triangles near lit candles!).

You can make whatever size triangle you prefer, but as a guideline I have drawn a template (fig. 59). Make sure you cut the card out accurately, particularly flaps C and D, or the triangle won't close properly.

You need: a piece of card in a colour of your choice (gold, silver, shiny red or black can look very striking); pencil; ruler; sheet of greaseproof paper; scissors; compass, protractor or saucer (to draw the curve); length of ribbon (approximately 16 cm (6¼ in)); strong stick or liquid adhesive; double-sided tape; invisible tape; materials to decorate.

With the outside facing up, trace the design onto greaseproof paper. Cut out the card (fig. 59a). Punch out the two holes (X and Y) taking great care to place them correctly (fig. 59b). The holes need to be in line with each other when folded over, but nearer the outside curve on flap D so that they overlap when the triangle is completed.

With the outside still face up, score (rule heavily with a pencil) lines A and B (fig. 59c). Fold them over sharply and then unfold. Using the compass, protractor or saucer, also score heavily curves C and D, and then gently fold them inwards (working from the centre to the edges) (fig. 59d). Lay the sheet flat again.

With the inside face up, take the thin strip of ribbon

On St Valentine's Day, don't wear your heart on your sleeve – seal one to a gift instead!

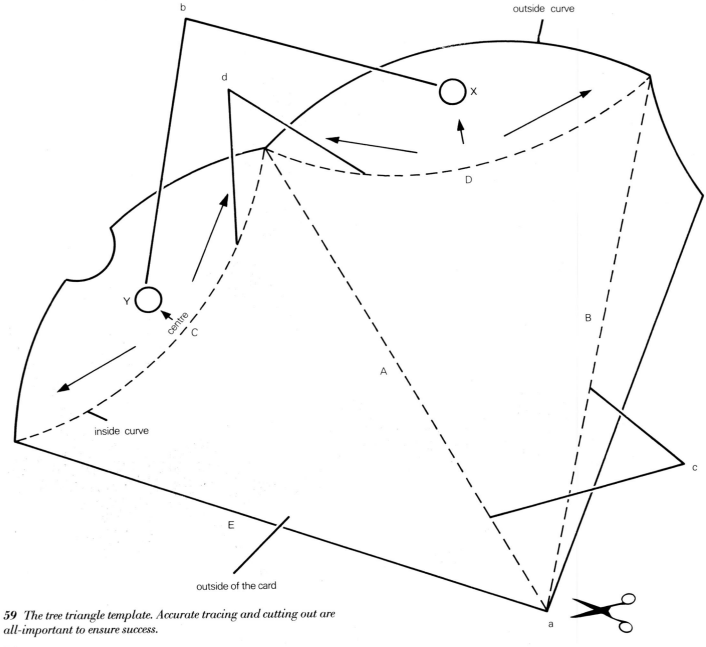

outside curve

b

d

X

D

Y

centre

C

inside curve

B

A

E

outside of the card

a

c

59 *The tree triangle template. Accurate tracing and cutting out are all-important to ensure success.*

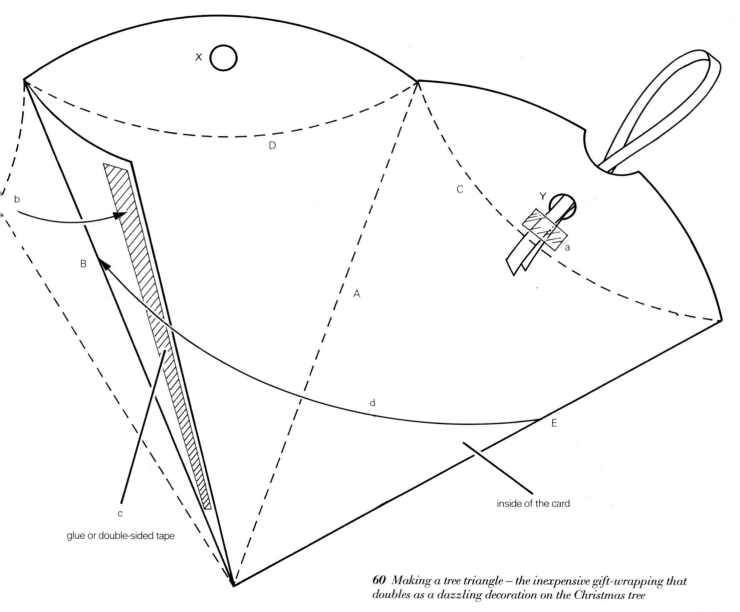

x

b

B

c

glue or double-sided tape

D

C

Y

a

A

d

E

inside of the card

60 Making a tree triangle – the inexpensive gift-wrapping that doubles as a dazzling decoration on the Christmas tree

Tree triangles (front left) and a garland of fruit (front centre) are just two ideas for a merry Christmas.

and fold it in half. Using invisible tape, seal the two ends to the inside below the punched hole Y (fig. 60a).

Fold in overlap B (fig. 60b). Run a strong adhesive or a strip of double-sided tape along the outside of B making sure you cover the full length (fig. 60c). Then fold along line A so that edge E lines up with B (fig. 60d).

With the ribbon facing you, fold in flap C. Push the ribbon through the other hole and press flap D over C.

Turn the triangle around and decorate the front. If you have some mini curl garland try entwining it with a length of ribbon. Then run a strip of double-sided tape down the centre of the front of the triangle and seal the decoration to it. Alternatively, cut out a shape from an old card, for example a robin, or make a ribbon decoration, or draw a name card and stick it to the front of the triangle using double-sided tape.

ACKNOWLEDGMENTS

My very sincere thanks to Keith Cavers for his excellent guidance and advice. Grateful thanks also to Gary Colet, Jack Pundick, Jessica and Simon Roland, Carol Tobias and especially Carine Kennedy and Beverlie Wine for their help in the testing of directions and the preparation of the manuscript.

The author and publishers would also like to thank the following for supplying materials used in photography:

For providing specialist papers

Paperchase
213 Tottenham Court Road
London, W1P 9AF

For providing materials used in the making up of cards and tags

Cowling & Wilcox Ltd
26/28 Broadwick Street
London, W1

Wheatsheaf Graphics
54 Baker Street
London, W1

For providing sequin scrap and lurex braid

Ells & Farrier Ltd
20 Princes Street
Hanover Square, London
W1R 8PH

For providing stickers

Action Tapes
Unit 5
Boundary Road
Brackley, Northants

Mrs Grossman's Paper Company (UK) Ltd
Millboard Road
Bourne End
Bucks, SL8 5XD

For providing wrapping paper

Apricot Designs
3 The Spires
Queens Road
Maidstone
Kent, ME16 0JE

Concertina Publications Ltd
19 Broad Court
London
WC2B 5QN

Courtier Fine Art Ltd
188 Goswell Road
London
EC1V 7DT

J Arthur Dixon
Forest Side
Newport
Isle of Wight
PO30 5QW

Elgin Court Designs Ltd
3 Shepherd Road
Gloucester, GL2 6EL

Gallery 5
121 King Street
London, W6 9JG

Gemma Designs Ltd
1 Towergate Industrial Park
Weyhill Road
Andover
Hampshire
SP10 3BB

Gordon Fraser Gallery Ltd
Eastcotts Road
Bedford
MK42 0JX

Graphiti
25a Market Place
Ripon
North Yorkshire

Greton Giftwrap
Enterprise House
Perry Road
Harlow
Essex
CM18 7PW

Italpapers
Arbour Farm
Wormingford Road
Fordham
Nr Colchester
Essex
CO6 3NS

Nigel Quiney Designs Ltd
30–31 Cloudesley Place
London
N1 0HZ

The Perfect Packaging Co
International House
Ordsall Lane
Salford
Manchester
M5 3HB

Popprint Products Ltd
2–4 Crescent Road
London
N22 4RS

Scandinavian Design Ltd
Penallta Industrial Estate
Ystrad Mynach
Hengoed
Mid Glamorgan
CF8 7UZ

Stop Press
3 The Spires
Queen's Road
Maidstone
Kent, ME16 0JE

Triangle Design Studios
202–208 New North Road
London, N1 7BL